OCT 21 1996

SOMALIA
The Missed Opportunities

SOMALIA
THE MISSED OPPORTUNITIES

Mohamed Sahnoun

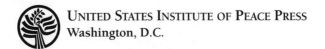

UNITED STATES INSTITUTE OF PEACE PRESS
Washington, D.C.

The views expressed in this book are those of the author alone. They do not necessarily reflect views of the United States Institute of Peace.

United States Institute of Peace
1550 M Street, N.W.
Washington, D.C. 20005

First published 1994

Printed in the United States of America

The paper used in this publication meets the minimum requirements of American National Standard for Information Sciences—Permanence of Paper for Printed Library Materials, ANSI Z39.48-1984.

Library of Congress Cataloging-in-Publication Data
Sahnoun, Mohamed.
    Somalia : the missed opportunities / by Mohamed Sahnoun.
      p. cm.
    Includes bibliographical references and index.
    ISBN 1-878379-35-6 (pbk. : acid-free paper)
    1. Somalia—Politics and government—1960– . 2. Insurgency—Somalia—History—20th century. 3. Clans—Somalia. 4. Maxamed Siyaad Barre, 1920– . I. Title.
DT407.S24 1994
967.7305—dc20   94-3624
                                                                      CIP

CONTENTS

PREFACE

GIVEN THE importance of the current debate on the effectiveness of international conflict resolution and the role of multilateral organizations, I felt it my duty to describe my experience as the UN special representative in Somalia in 1992. It is my sincere wish that some lessons can be drawn from this limited but significant experience in Somalia, at the very beginning of the UN involvement in that country.

I lived in the Horn of Africa, or more precisely in Addis Ababa, Ethiopia, for almost a decade, in the late 1960s and early '70s, and I am very attached to the region. I was the deputy secretary-general of the Organization of African Unity, in charge of political affairs, and therefore oversaw some of the conflict situations in the continent and particularly in the Horn. The problems of the subregion were among the most serious issues for the OAU, which was often asked to use its good offices to reduce the prevailing tension between Somalia and its neighbors. Furthermore, the Horn of Africa is often subject to successive and long-lasting droughts that affect deeply the livelihood and the social and political environment of the inhabitants.

When the secretary-general of the United Nations, Boutros Boutros-Ghali, asked me if I would be willing to undertake a fact-finding mission in Somalia in March 1992, I accepted without hesitation. I had already been informed by some friends in the region about the humanitarian tragedy that was unfolding in parts of the country, and I was eager to find out for myself the extent of the tragedy and to assess how the international community should respond.

As our plane landed on a small strip to the north of Mogadishu—the main airport being closed—and as we drove slowly towards the city, I could not believe my eyes. I had visited Somalia before, and what I was seeing now was a total disaster. I describe later in this book some characteristics of this disaster. But here I was, alone, without support staff, and I was being asked to undertake the task of working out a plan whereby the United Nations could facilitate the cessation of hostilities between the Somali factions, promote reconciliation, and provide urgently needed humanitarian assistance.

I reported to the secretary-general about this appalling situation and how we urgently needed to put in place a real rescue operation of a greater magnitude than the one organized at the time of the Ethiopian famine in the early 1980s or in the "Biafran" war in the late '60s.

After the Security Council confirmed the appointment of a special representative in April 1992, I officially began my mission as head of the United Nations Operation in Somalia (UNOSOM). It was still largely a one-person operation. I had to rely on a small staff put at our disposal by UNICEF and shared with the coordinator for humanitarian assistance, David Bassiouny. It took several weeks before the headquarters in New York finally designated Livio Bota, from the UN office in Geneva, and Leonard Kapungu, from the Political Department, to be my assistants, and some more weeks before a support staff could join us.

UNOSOM had in fact taken a real shape only by the time I finally left Somalia, that is, six months after my appointment. But this did not discourage our small team. Relying largely on a few wonderful nongovernmental organizations and on the good relationship we established with the Somali people, we were, I believe, able to create a good, friendly, and warm atmosphere that helped us resolve many intractable issues. The cease-fire was largely respected; the ports and airports of Mogadishu, Kismayu, and elsewhere were opened; and a chain of solidarity with the Somali people began gradually to materialize. I wish we had been allowed to continue . . .

We owe much of this success to the mass media, to which I want to pay a special tribute. Beginning in July, when the security situation had improved, I invited and helped the media, which until then had followed events mostly out of Nairobi, to make their way to several parts of Somalia.

The media reported on the situation with remarkable accuracy and speed, and this media coverage clearly initiated a substantial increase in emergency relief, including a direct airlift operation out of Kenya and Djibouti organized by the United States and other governments. The articles by Jane Perlez, *New York Times* correspondent, played a key role in arousing world attention to the plight of the Somali people. These articles were followed by other television and press reports, including one by *60 Minutes*, for which I was blamed by UN headquarters because of its critical assessment of the UN agencies' role.

I have written this testimony from the viewpoint of someone who believes strongly in intervention through mediation and prevention. Prevention can assume different forms, including pressure and sanctions. We have not yet explored all avenues open to prevention, especially by regional organizations. I have been recently involved in mediation on behalf of the Organization of African Unity to prevent large-scale conflict in the Congo. I believe we have been successful, because the situation is largely stabilized. Elections were held and both the government majority and the opposition are cooperating within the parliament. Problems can still arise, and there might be a need to buttress and consolidate this achievement through a large economic development program. But it is an example of successful preventive diplomacy. It could be done still in Burundi, Zaire, and so on; and it could have been achieved in Somalia, Bosnia, and Rwanda.

This is my conviction. Conflicts are not necessarily endemic. The ingredients of the crisis, which are often there anyway, gather, however, like clouds before the storm when circumstances dictate for them to do so! We should draw lessons from past experience on how some aggravating factors such as arms supply (for example, in Somalia and Rwanda) and the environment compound and ignite conflicts and wars. If this book can make some contribution to the current debate and help improve policies for the prevention and resolution of conflicts, it will have achieved its aim. It has no other purpose.

A final note. I must express my deepest gratitude to all those who helped me in Somalia and to others who provided their support and encouraged me in my task. I also would like to thank all those at the United States Institute of Peace who provided me with a warm refuge after

Somalia and an atmosphere for reflection and exchange, while I was a visiting distinguished fellow in the Jennings Randolph Program for International Peace at the Institute.

I should add that the preparation of this book was accomplished with the assistance of a number of people, among whom I would like to thank especially Joe Klaits, Robert Oakley, Dan O'Connor, Dan Snodderly, and Robin Wright.

INTRODUCTION

SINCE THE end of the Second World War the world community has been largely powerless when confronted with local crises. Internal conflicts have usually been perceived as occurring within sovereign states and therefore not warranting outside intervention. Most of the time serious opportunities to mediate and check crises at an early stage have gone unheeded. Occasionally, when crises have reached important dimensions and affected large populations, hasty and ill-prepared emergency relief operations have been put in place while a few timid attempts at reconciliation have been initiated. Even in most of the recent cases, such as Rwanda, Angola, Mozambique, Liberia, Somalia, Cambodia, Afghanistan, and Bosnia, the international community and the United Nations (UN) have begun to take serious initiatives only when large-scale civil wars have engulfed the countries and human tragedies have become overwhelming.

Most of these internal conflicts result from a number of factors, such as the legacy of colonial times, as, for instance, in border issues; the context of the Cold War, in which corrupt or authoritarian rule was tolerated in the name of confronting communism, on the one hand, or capitalism, on the other; and the failure of many of Third World elites to cope with the political, economic, and sociological challenges of the new era. With the end of the Cold War and the proliferation of new challenges—such as the environment—internal conflicts are bound to continue to erupt worldwide for the foreseeable future. Apart from their impact on the local population, such conflicts might present a serious threat to peace and security in entire regions of the world. Therefore, it is important to explore ways of checking these internal conflicts before they become unmanageable, before their impact on innocent people becomes unbearable, and before they disrupt regional stability. Early intervention, both political and humanitarian, can save hundreds of thousands of lives and avoid a disaster that might affect a whole generation of people in many ways.

The framers of the UN Charter were keen to offer the international community a document that would provide means for peaceful solutions to all disputes, including conflicts within states that could become a threat to international peace and security. Only in exceptional situations does the charter advocate the use of force, and even then it clearly spells out a number of measures—such as imposing economic sanctions—to be taken first.

Article 33 of the charter, which is central to the whole architecture of the document, reflects the framers' preference for peaceful solutions:

> The parties to any dispute, the continuance of which is likely to endanger the maintenance of international peace and security, shall, first of all, seek a solution by negotiation, enquiry, mediation, conciliation, arbitration, judicial settlement, resort to regional agencies or arrangements, or other peaceful means of their own choice.
>
> The Security Council shall, when it deems necessary, call upon the parties to settle their dispute by such means.

Chapter VIII of the charter, which deals in three long articles with regional arrangements, underlines further that member states should make every effort to achieve peaceful settlement of disputes through regional organizations before referring them to the Security Council. The UN and regional organizations should cooperate to put in place a monitoring system in different regions of the world that can alert UN headquarters to an impending crisis and suggest ways to avert a larger conflict. Preventive action must rely on permanent structures and adequate human resources. Statesmen experienced in brokering peace should be available on short notice to undertake specific mediation operations as special envoys of regional organizations and, when necessary, of the UN.

In addition to the members of the UN, the secretary-general himself is authorized to bring "to the attention of the Security Council any matter which in his opinion may threaten the maintenance of international peace and security" (Article 99 of the charter). This authorization has hardly been used by recent secretaries-general. Yet it is clear that by referring to "any matter" here the drafters of the charter broadened the scope of the secretary-general's mandate to allow him to determine whether and when specific situations warrant the attention of the Security Council and to address such matters to the council. This article implies that the secretary-general is entitled to make the necessary investigations and to assess the means of resolving an issue well before it evolves into a dangerous conflict.

It is my belief that if the international community had intervened earlier and more effectively in Somalia, much of the catastrophe that has unfolded could have been avoided. In theory, there should have been no shortage of actors who could have intervened to mediate the conflicts that engulfed Somalia. Somalia is a member of the League of Arab States, the Organization of African Unity (OAU), and the Islamic Conference. During the Carter and Reagan administrations, Somalia was also a close ally of the United States, receiving hundreds of millions of dollars in American economic and military assistance. Somalia also maintained good relations with the former colonial powers Great Britain and Italy, two important members of the European Community. Finally, Somalia was, of course, a member of the UN. Any one of these actors could have offered its services as a mediator or supported the mediation efforts timidly undertaken at various times. Sadly, none of these nations or institutions, all supposedly friends of Somalia and its people, moved seriously to help the country in its hour of need in a timely and efficient way. When the international community finally did begin to intervene in early 1992, hundreds of thousands of lives had already been lost.

In the following pages I will look at the Somali case, which provides specific examples of how the failure of the international community to intervene in different phases of a crisis can be detrimental and lead to further deterioration. I will examine the relationship between intervention and sovereignty—how there is no basic contradiction between the two if certain precautionary measures are taken—and attempt to assess some of the reasons for the failure of the UN to take adequate and timely action to prevent conflict.

SOMALIA
The Missed Opportunities

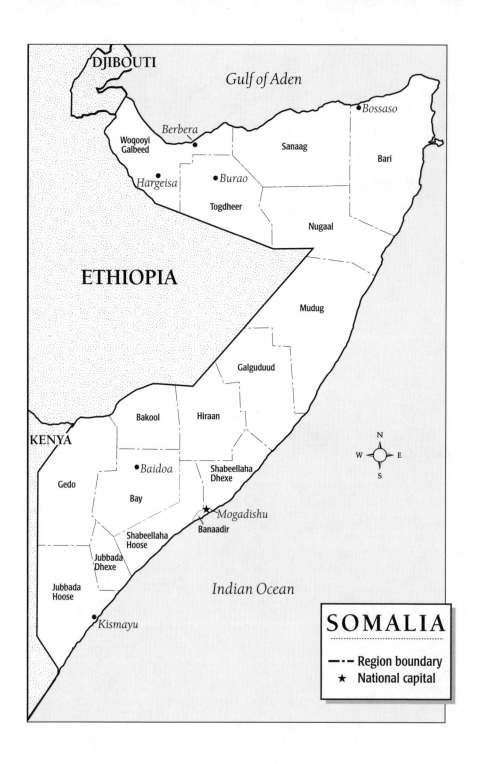

1
Opportunities for Preventive Diplomacy

*T*HREE SPECIFIC instances in the case of Somalia represent classic crisis situations in which the international community might be called upon to intervene. A preventive approach in such a case has a fairly good chance of success without great expense, and without the need for a large military presence.

The Uprising in the North

Although Somalia had known several periods of unrest since its independence in 1960, the first serious crisis was an uprising in the North in May and June 1988 that ultimately led to the disintegration of the country.[1] The uprising was fueled both by clan-based rivalries and by political and economic considerations. Inhabitants of the northern part of Somalia, home of the large Issaq clan, as well as smaller clans, came to resent the leadership of the southern groups, especially the Marehan, a subclan of the Darod clan. The northerners consider the Marehan to have monopolized political power since Siad Barre, a Marehan, took over in 1969. Up to the spring of 1988, through skillful maneuvering and repression, Siad Barre had managed to stifle the clan conflicts in Somalia, despite the fact that the top echelons of his government consisted mostly of members of his small subclan.[2]

The northern region produced surplus livestock that accounted for the largest share of Somali export earnings in 1983.[3] The northerners felt a sense of injustice because the resources of the region were not benefiting them primarily and because there was no equitable regional economic development. They were also frustrated in their desire to maintain close ties with the populations across the border in both Ethiopia and Djibouti; rather than facilitating institutional contacts between these populations, the Mogadishu government used the issue in a demagogic fashion to exacerbate tensions with its neighbors.

The inhabitants of the northern regions clearly perceived themselves to be wronged and without the possibility of democratic redress. The uprising was led by the Somali National Movement (SNM), an opposition group rooted mainly in the North. The SNM forces met with initial success, attacking the two biggest cities, Burao and Hargeisa.[4] Governmental forces, unable to prevent this uprising that resulted from long-standing grievances, used aircraft and heavy weapons in a bloody effort to repress the civilian population.[5] Siad Barre's forces destroyed many of the cities and much of the infrastructure of the area. An estimated 5,000 civilian members of the Issaq clan were killed in May 1988 alone. Thousands more people lost their lives and many more were injured over the following months, as both insurgency and repression spread throughout the region.[6]

At the time, Amnesty International denounced the systematic torture of prisoners by the government security forces, and human rights organizations around the world protested the repression.[7] Africa Watch called for an "international outcry against the killing of thousands of civilians in the civil war in Somalia."[8] In fact, the violence in Somalia was documented in a number of separate reports, two of them conducted by the U.S. government.[9] The world community was clearly witnessing a serious crisis in which a large population faced the dire consequences of what was to be a civil war. One would expect that in the absence of a democratic mechanism allowing for corrective measures, the international community would come to the rescue of the victimized population. It did not, and this represents the *first missed opportunity*.

The Manifesto

In May 1990, exactly two years after the beginning of the uprising in the North and as armed opposition spread significantly to other regions of the country, a manifesto calling for a national conference to reconcile the various movements and ethnic groups was published in Mogadishu. The manifesto was signed by 144 well-known and moderate political leaders. One, a former government official named Ahmed Darman, noted that the manifesto's signatories included intellectuals, business people, and tradesmen as well as officials from the Siad Barre and previous regimes. The group took what constituted, for the period, a courageous step by calling for a peaceful end to the war.[10]

The group blamed the government for the atrocities committed during the uprising, suggested the abolition of repressive laws as a sign of the government's sincerity, and called for a multiparty system, constitutional changes, and a national reconciliation conference that would form a caretaker government and prepare elections. To organize the conference, the group proposed a thirteen-person committee headed by the country's first president, Adam Abdullah Osman, and the former parliament president, Sheikh Mukhtar Mohamed Hussein.[11]

It should be emphasized here that the members of the manifesto group, who were for the most part living in Mogadishu, had every reason to fear for their lives.[12] They openly confronted a regime that thoroughly resented such a move as an affront to its authority. The conscience of Somalia was clearly seeking to impress on the government as well as on the insurgency groups the need to stop the fighting and begin negotiations. Abdul Mohammed, who was executive director of the Inter-African Group based in Addis Ababa and who was close to the Ethiopian government, suggested in July 1990 that the UN appoint a special envoy to conduct shuttle diplomacy in the Horn of Africa.[13]

The Italian and Egyptian governments attempted to convene a conference between the opposition groups and the government in December 1990. At a Rome meeting on November 15, 1990, some opposition groups tentatively agreed to attend the December conference, but others suspected that the move was an attempt to salvage the Siad Barre regime. They were reluctant to attend, and the matter was not pursued.

There were, of course, other limited diplomatic démarches and protests. U.S. Secretary of State James Baker stated in a meeting with the Somali prime minister that U.S. bilateral assistance to Somalia would be suspended until the Mogadishu government demonstrated proper respect for human rights. Military assistance had been suspended since July 1988 by the State Department under pressure from the House Foreign Affairs Committee,[14] although military support materials continued to be delivered through mid-1989. Economic support funds totaling $20 million were frozen in June 1989.[15] These moves, although limited, were significant, but few other governments took even such modest steps.

There was no concerted action on the part of the international community. In fact, the UN began to evacuate its personnel from Hargeisa and elsewhere in Somalia as early as the summer of 1988 for safety reasons. The UN High Commission for Refugees was in the middle of an embarrassing situation following charges of infighting and widescale corruption in its program. Neither the UN nor the regional organizations were providing any leadership for serious mediation efforts, and the fragile and isolated endeavors of a few governments could have no impact. While the world watched, Siad Barre's government responded to the manifesto by arresting many of its signatories, including the former president of Somalia, Adam Abdullah Osman. The international community and the UN should have seized the opportunity provided by the manifesto appeal to offer its good offices for mediation. This was the *second missed opportunity*.

The Fall of the Siad Barre Government

The conflict was now spreading throughout the country. Siad Barre appointed new prime ministers and promised democracy; at the same time, he unleashed one of the worst reprisals ever witnessed against his own people. The Somali Parliament "approved a new constitution promising free speech and multiparty elections"; Siad Barre insisted, however, that the changes would not take place until after a national referendum, the timing of which was unspecified.[16] As the situation deteriorated, the government began pushing for talks with the rebel movements, but press reports indicated that as the insurgency closed in on Mogadishu in December 1990, hundreds of people were killed.[17] On January 5, 1991, in the midst of the final preparations for Desert Storm, the United States had to dispatch helicopters from two amphibious carriers near Somalia as part of the Desert Shield deployment to rescue Americans and other foreigners from Mogadishu.[18] Siad Barre and his supporters finally fled Mogadishu on January 27, 1991.

Somalia was then without a government, and the major insurgent movements controlled the capital. The appointment by some manifesto leaders of Ali Mahdi, a well-known personality from the United Somali Congress (USC) and a signatory himself of the manifesto, as provisional president was rejected by other groups.[19] Ali Mahdi was a member of the Abgal subclan of the Hawiye, the dominant clan of the USC. His chief rival, Mohammed Farah Aideed, also hailed from the Hawiye clan, but from the Habar-Gedir subclan.[20] These two subclans together dominated the Mogadishu area. Despite tensions, a precarious cease-fire prevailed in Mogadishu at this stage. In February 1991 Ali Mahdi's government invited all of the armed groups to a national reconciliation conference in Mogadishu. Some of the groups refused to come, and after two postponements and no outside support, the idea of a conference was abandoned.[21]

A few timid attempts at mediation were made by some governments in the region.[22] The UN, however, was totally absent. It had already evacuated all of its staff from Somalia.[23] Some nongovernmental organizations (NGOs), especially the International Committee of the Red Cross (ICRC), were able to maintain their presence despite enormous difficulties. The only functioning hospital in Mogadishu was run by an international NGO called SOS.[24] Another NGO, Médecins sans Frontières, maintained a surgical and medical team in Mogadishu despite great risks. The organization reportedly provided 80 percent of the drugs and medical supplies used by all health care facilities in Mogadishu in 1991.[25] The United States increased its humanitarian aid to Somalia by $19 million "because of the United Nations's refusal to organize significant aid to the beleaguered country,"[26] but saw no need to become involved in finding a political solution to the conflict. The Cold War–era military facility at Berbera turned out to be completely unnecessary for Desert Shield deployment.[27]

There was some movement toward convening a reconciliation conference through Ethiopian and Eritrean mediation. The two neighbors hoped to have a broad-based conference that would include the military forces on the ground. This initiative came to nothing, however, because of lack of international and regional support.[28]

One serious attempt at reconciliation was undertaken by the Djibouti government from July 15 to 21, 1991. With the support of some regional governments, a meeting of several parties was held at Djibouti and a partial agreement was reached on the steps to be taken to promote peace and democracy. Unfortunately, the results of this conference were not endorsed by all the parties. Among the problems that hampered the meeting were the following:

1. The delegates to the conference had only limited control of the forces on the ground.
2. The conference was attended by movements based in some regions of the country, but not all.
3. Procedures established for enforcing the cease-fire remained vague.
4. The problem of how to deal with ex-president Siad Barre was still perceived as a military issue, and his clan (or his political base) was ignored.[29]

Clearly, the organizers of the conference lacked experience and could not exert enough pressure to get all parties to the conflict to agree. The confirmation of Ali Mahdi as president for two years, a move recommended by the conference, quickly became a problem. His rival in the USC, Aideed, would not agree to abide by the conference results. Another agreement signed on August 6, 1991, was thought to have smoothed over the problems left from the conference, but this agreement did not hold for long, and violent clashes broke out between the two camps.[30]

The government of Djibouti had requested the support of the UN, which refused with no explanation except that the matter was too complicated.[31] Had the UN, together with the regional organizations, been involved in preparing this conference, the reconciliation process could have gotten off to a good start. Even though the negotiations might have been long and arduous, international pressure would have ensured that all parties were committed to the results. This conference was the *third missed opportunity.*

Because of the failure of this attempt at reconciliation and the absence of any important alternative, the Somali factions were left to themselves, and soon intraclan fighting began in Mogadishu. That was the worst part of the civil war. Fighting between the two factions of the USC broke out on November 17, 1991. This battle laid to waste large areas of the city in November and December 1991.[32] Estimates of the number of deaths through March 1992 ranged as high as 30,000. It was estimated that 500,000 people were without basic services.[33] Clan fighting also spread to other regions of Somalia, including Somaliland. Siad Barre's forces succeeded in capturing Kismayu in the South and were approaching Mogadishu.[34] The dangerous conditions forced the remaining humanitarian organizations to briefly shut down their operations in Somalia.[35]

2
The UN Role in Humanitarian Assistance

*H*AVING SEEN the development of the situation in the absence of a UN role, let us now examine what happened when the UN finally decided to concern itself with the matter.

Outgoing UN Secretary-General Javier Pérez de Cuéllar decided in December 1991 to take a more active role in resolving the conflict. When the Security Council adopted its first resolution on Somalia, Resolution 733, on January 23, 1992, the situation was almost hopeless. The resolution called for a total arms embargo and urged the conflicting parties to agree to a cease-fire and to promote the process of reconciliation in Somalia. It also requested increased humanitarian aid to the country and asked the parties to ensure the safety of those delivering aid.[36] In February 1992 talks between warring factions were held in New York under the auspices of the UN, the League of Arab States, the OAU, and the Islamic Conference. The parties agreed on an immediate cessation of hostilities and the maintenance of a cease-fire.[37] The New York talks were billed as the beginning of a more active UN role in Somalia.[38]

When I arrived in Mogadishu in March 1992 on a fact-finding mission, the city was nearly deserted. Most people had fled to the surrounding areas, where they lived in the worst of conditions and many faced death by starvation. Despite the cease-fire agreement, fighting still occurred periodically around Mogadishu. These skirmishes seemed grotesque in view of the tragedy and chaos in the country as a whole. At least 300,000 people had died of hunger and hunger-related disease, and thousands more were casualties of the repression and the civil war. Seventy percent of the country's livestock had been lost, and the farming areas had been devastated, compelling the farming population to seek refuge in remote areas or across the border in refugee camps.[39] Some 500,000 people were in camps in Ethiopia, Kenya, and Djibouti.[40] More than 3,000—mostly women, children, and old men—were dying daily from starvation. That was the tragic situation in Somalia at the beginning of 1992.[41]

After the Security Council adopted its second and third resolutions on Somalia, on March 17 and April 24, 1992, respectively, great hopes were raised. The third resolution, which established the United Nations Operation in Somalia (UNOSOM), requested the secretary-general "to facilitate an immediate and effective cessation of hostilities and the maintenance of a cease-fire throughout the country in order to promote the process of reconciliation and political settlement in Somalia and to provide urgent humanitarian assistance." It also "[decided] to establish . . . a Committee of the Security Council . . . to recommend appropriate measures in response to violations of the general and complete embargo on all deliveries of weapons and military equipment to Somalia" and "[called] upon the international community to support, with financial and other resources, the implementation of the 90-day Plan of Action for Emergency Humanitarian Assistance to Somalia."

The UNOSOM team, of which I was the head, had limited resources with which to work, yet we were expected to help supply food, provide administrative expertise and coordination for relief operations, help restore infrastructure, and, of course, mediate all kinds of clan disputes. There was no military option at this initial stage. The UN mission had to rely to a large degree on moral suasion to get things done.[42]

Skirmishes in Mogadishu were diminishing. There were no large-scale confrontations. The Somali people viewed the arrival of the UNOSOM team as a sign of outside interest in their fate. Most Somalis still could not comprehend why the world community had deserted them when they overthrew their dictator, Siad Barre, in January 1991.[43] Above all, they could not understand why the UN and all its agencies had kept a distant and suspicious stance toward Somalia when their needs were so obvious. They could not but compare the behavior of the UN with that of the charitable institutions and NGOs that had provided essential relief and come to the rescue of the starving and the sick. The means of the NGOs were limited, but their goodwill and their courage were admirable. It was largely thanks to the NGOs that the population began to gradually return to Mogadishu, as well as to other cities and villages, in March 1992. Despite their deep-seated grievances and distrust, the Somali leaders agreed to deal with the UN. As early as March 1992, all of them agreed to a UN mediation effort and accepted, in principle, the deployment of security forces for the protection of emergency relief efforts.

All of these leaders, however, insisted on the need to launch an urgent and large humanitarian assistance operation as well as a recovery program. They were very concerned that they would lose control of some of the young militia, who might join other unruly youths already engaged in looting. Since arms and ammunition were easily available, this was a justifiable primary concern. It was estimated that more than 40,000 weapons had been abandoned by the former Somali army as the civil war reached its peak in January 1992 and the troops were forced to disband.[44] Many Somali leaders had requested UN assistance in disarming the population. However, the Somalis would voluntarily bring in their weapons only if offered a food basket or other form of inducement such as temporary employment. None of these were available.

It should be emphasized that some faction leaders did not hesitate to condone banditry and looting just to retain their authority. Even Aideed, considered the strongest of the militia leaders, had trouble controlling his fighters and ensuring public safety in areas he controlled.[45] He occasionally covered up or condoned looting undertaken by his allies.

Had the UN's assistance, both military and humanitarian, been forthcoming in the way and at the level expected by relief workers and Somalis, it would have greatly contributed to an atmosphere propitious to dialogue and compromise. As I stated at the time, "The provision of humanitarian assistance and the maintenance of the cease-fire are closely linked. We need both at the same time. People are in terrible need of food and medical assistance, and if we fail to address that situation, it will certainly worsen and there might be a flare-up of hostilities."[46] The UN again proved unequal to the task.[47] Not only was the UN assistance program very limited, it was also so slowly and inadequately delivered that it became counterproductive. Fighting erupted over the meager food supplied and introduced new elements of animosity and violence. UN World Food

Program head Trevor Page noted that the problems got out of hand in Somalia "because we've let things simmer without paying attention" and that "because of the disorganization of the United Nations, less than a third of the food that is needed had been delivered."[48]

While the ICRC and all NGOs—especially SOS, Médecins sans Frontières, International Medical Corps (IMC), Save the Children, Irish Concern, and CARE—did their utmost to enhance their programs and ventured deep inside Somalia to provide emergency relief to the population despite tremendous dangers and difficulties, some UN agencies were arguing that the security situation precluded their presence or, at best, permitted the presence of only a small staff.[49] As one source noted, "The non-governmental relief agencies remain deeply critical of the United Nations for not doing more."[50]

My argument was in favor of breaking the vicious circle. The scarcity of food exacerbated the atmosphere of insecurity that already prevailed within the country. Bureaucratic haggling and obstructions within the UN relief agencies hampered efforts to feed the hungry. In an urgent report filed in June 1992, I wrote the following:

> Somalia is today a country without central, regional or local administration, and without services. No electricity, no communication, no transport, no school, no health services! Yet, the support for relief efforts has been disappointing. The ICRC and UNICEF continue to make a sterling contribution with the support of international NGOs. Over one million children are at risk, due to malnutrition, and will become the first casualties, in large numbers, if supplementary feeding programmes are not put in place or accelerated within the next few weeks.

> Most of the population have no money to buy food from the market since virtually all economic activities have been disrupted by the war. Some 4,500,000 people are in urgent need of food. Thousands of people are in camps, others in small groups isolated and desolate, while hundreds of thousands of refugees are in border areas with Kenya, Ethiopia and Djibouti.

> An absence of food breeds insecurity which, in turn, causes instability leading to starvation, suffering and disease. Breaking this diabolical and vicious cycle may be the key to resolving the intricate social and political problems in Somalia.

> A minimum of 50,000 MT [metric tons] of different food items is needed urgently. Less than half this amount has been pledged. The shortfall must

be met immediately if a general catastrophe is to be avoided. The arrival at Mogadishu port recently of two ships with a total of 12,000 MT of wheat arranged by the WFP [World Food Program], and of a Saudi ship with 4,000 MT of food supply was certainly welcomed. Until then, ICRC was the only organization which was able to send a number of small ships along the coast of Somalia. However, if these are not followed, very quickly, by other ships bringing foods to other ports such as Bossaso, Berbera and Kismayu, the traumatic situation will have profound effects on a whole generation of Somalis.

Additional supplementary feeding commodities are required immediately for use in therapeutic feeding centers for children operating in Mogadishu and a few other towns. Supplementary feeding will improve the nutritional condition of malnourished children, help stabilize the health and nutrition status of those already at risk and, hopefully, reduce the extremely high rate of death among children. UNIMIX, dried skim milk (DSM), sugar, oil, and high energy biscuits is the combination identified for this vital nutritional rescue plan. Except for some modest contributions from UNICEF and Save the Children Fund, there is yet no definite pledge or commitment from other sources for such commodities.

The situation in the health sector is grave. Of the estimated 70 hospitals in Somalia in 1988, only 15 remain partially operational today, and are totally dependent on external assistance. Most of the hospitals have no water, no electricity, no drugs or even the most basic medical equipment. Malaria, tuberculosis and vaccination programmes were interrupted with the collapse of the primary health care structure. The urgent need in this sector is the provision of a basic minimum of medical supplies as well as materials for the repair and rehabilitation of hospitals, and Mother and Child Health (MCH) clinics.

A potential disaster looms large as the sanitary situation throughout the country continues to deteriorate, posing a major threat to public health. Streets are blocked with rubbish. With the onset of the rain, the situation could deteriorate even more rapidly. Potable water supply has disappeared along with all other health and social services, with the collapse of civil infrastructure. Large numbers of people are at risk of epidemics. An indeterminate number have already died. The two-year old drought has further compounded this situation. Fuel, pumps, piping and technical assistance are required urgently to help rehabilitate water sources and to restart water and environmental sanitation programs on an emergency basis. Some water rehabilitation programmes have been initiated.

Livestock has been, and remains central to the economy of Somalia and its people, yet cattle continue to die of disease by the thousands in the absence of veterinary services and medicines. A programme must be implemented immediately to vaccinate cattle, primarily against rinderpest, and to re-establish quarantine centers in all of the major trading ports. This is an effort to eradicate disease among cattle as a first step towards revitalizing existing herds, and trade in livestock.

A combination of drought and war has had a devastating effect on agriculture, in particular on cereal production. Some 35,000 MT of seeds is required urgently to restart agricultural production. The international community will also need to assist in providing hand tools and other equipment. Coastal fishing communities in the north-east are lacking everything from nets, to engines, spare parts, fuel and refrigeration equipment.

Over 300,000 people are now registered as refugees in Kenya with a daily increase of 1,000. Sites now identified and officially allocated by the Government of Kenya have a capacity for 130,000. In the absence of a new and bold approach, there will be some 500,000 refugees in Kenya alone by 1993. Large numbers of refugees are also in Ethiopia, Djibouti and other States in the Horn of Africa.[51]

The central problem was that between January and July 1992 the UN agencies made little headway in creating distribution networks for food and in providing sufficient food deliveries. Despite repeated visits by technical assessment teams sent by different UN headquarters, very little got done on the ground in Somalia. The general assessment of food requirements for the whole country, including refugees, was a minimum of 50,000 MT per month; by this reckoning, the requirement for the six-month period from January through June would have amounted to 300,000 MT.

By mid-July the World Food Program had delivered, by its own admission, 18,857 MT of the 68,388 MT it had pledged in January.[52] This total consisted of 5,000 MT of wheat distributed in Mogadishu in late May, 7,000 MT of wheat distributed partly in Mogadishu and partly in Baidoa and Goher in June, and 5,500 MT of maize and 1,400 MT of beans in Mogadishu in July. Other UN agencies fared no better in this emergency relief operation in the first six months of 1992. In fact, most of them did not even maintain offices in Somalia; their representatives preferred to remain in Nairobi or Djibouti.

By comparison, between February and June 1992 the ICRC brought a total of 53,900 MT of food into Somalia through twenty different entry points, by sea, by air, and overland across the Kenya-Somalia border. The ICRC operated 400 kitchens, feeding more than 600,000 people in Mogadishu and six other towns. These community kitchens provided up to two cooked meals daily. The ICRC also handled the distribution of food to several hospitals in various cities and sustained four daily rotations of airlift delivery from Mombasa, Kenya, to Mogadishu, Belet Uen, and Baidoa. Most of the U.S. food sent to Somalia was handled by the ICRC.[53]

As the situation deteriorated in the summer of 1992 Secretary-General Boutros Boutros-Ghali proposed that another technical team be sent to Somalia. The Security Council supported his decision on July 27, 1992. The team visited Somalia from August 6 to 15, 1992, and the secretary-general submitted his report on August 24, 1992. In that report the secretary-general stated that the efforts of the ninety-day plan as well as the Special Emergency Program for the Horn of Africa were "in no way adequate to meet the overall needs of the Somali people. Present estimates, which may be conservative, indicate that as many as 4.5 million people are in desperate need of food and other assistance." The secretary-general further stated, "The immediate need is to break this vicious cycle. There must then be a comprehensive programme of action covering humanitarian relief, the cessation of hostilities, the reduction of organized and unorganized violence, and national reconciliation."[54]

In the face of this tragic situation I made an urgent appeal to donor countries to directly involve themselves in the delivery of food to Somalia through airlift operations.[55] On October 12, 1992, the donor countries, UN agencies, the ICRC, and NGOs met in Geneva and approved a one-hundred-day plan for accelerated relief deliveries to Somalia, which would replace the ninety-day plan of April 1992.

3

The UNOSOM Strategy

WHEN UNOSOM began its mission in April 1992, it was clear that Somali society had largely broken down and only a few safeguards remained on which the UNOSOM team could rely. What sustained our hope was the encouragement we had received from the elders in all regions as well as some former social, political, and administrative officials, including former police officers, and women leaders at both the national and community levels. These leaders approached us sometimes with tears in their eyes, offering to work closely with the UN to bring Somalia out of the mess it was in.

Despite previous bitter experience, all of them had consented to work with the UN and regional organizations for a comprehensive solution. The interim president of Somalia, Ali Mahdi, whose faction (the USC Manifesto Group) was in control in north Mogadishu, agreed to resign his position as acting president as soon as a meeting with other Somali leaders could be arranged. This agreement was important for progress, given the hostility toward him or, more precisely, toward his claim to be head of state.

The UNOSOM team pursued a strategy of putting the clan system to work for Somalia. Agreements among local elders helped to gradually reduce the fighting and allow food deliveries into the interior of the country. After arduous discussions and with the help of the elders, I persuaded Ali Mahdi, Aideed, and other faction leaders to allow the deployment of 500 UN peacekeepers in Mogadishu. Despite recurrent problems, the port was open and distribution through it was established.

Although insisting on their wish to secede from Somalia, the leaders of the SNM in the Northwest and the elders in Somaliland had not ruled out a discussion with the other Somali movements and accepted our advice that they should seek, as we put it, a "divorce by consent." Our meetings in Burao, Hargeisa, and Berbera drew large gatherings of community leaders and elders and, despite heated debate, remained friendly and constructive. Very often the leaders asked us to speak to their people directly to explain this concept of "divorce by consent."

The UNOSOM team's meetings in Kismayu had established very solid relations with a number of new leaders supported by the elders of southern Somalia. They were eager to join a peace forum convened, as we suggested, by the UN, the OAU, the Arab League, and the Islamic Conference, similar to conferences held in West Africa to help identify and promote new leadership that could become a credible alternative to the faction leaders. This was important for some populations in the South because they had been associated with the former president, Siad Barre, and they were eager to distance themselves from him.

The leadership in the Northeast and the elders of the area had, probably more than any others, committed themselves to cooperate fully with the UN. The UNOSOM team met with them on several occasions and invited to the discussions representatives of the society as a whole, including women, merchants, intellectuals, and members of youth associations. Our hope was to establish the Northeast as a model for the other regions of Somalia. Consensus prevailed in the region among the different clans and subclans, and UNOSOM's suggestions for organizing the local and regional administrations were being actively discussed and gradually implemented. But everything was missing. No infrastructure whatsoever was available. Despite our pressing appeals to UN agencies to have some presence in Bossaso and Garoe and to provide some assistance, at least to the displaced people in the area, we received only pledges and promises. It became difficult for me, as head of UNOSOM, to revisit the people there because we were not able to deliver the UNOSOM part of any agreement entered into with the local communities.

By the middle of October 1992, all faction leaders of the different regions and community elders had given their assent for a national conference whose objective would be to exchange views on the process of national reconciliation. The president of Ethiopia, Meles Zinawi, acting as president of a community set up by the heads of state of the Horn of

Africa (Ethiopia, Eritrea, Djibouti, Kenya, and Sudan) to deal with Somalia, proposed to hold this conference in Addis Ababa. (I want to underline here the role played by the president of Ethiopia and his colleagues in fully supporting my efforts and in appointing a working subcommittee headed by a junior minister in the foreign ministry, Lissan Johanes, to follow up on our joint endeavors to organize this process of national reconciliation.) I discussed the date with UN Secretary-General Boutros Boutros-Ghali, who favored early January 1993 so that he could personally attend.

The heads of state of the Horn of Africa had previously expressed disappointment that the UN did not support some of their moves toward Somalia and that the organization seemed reluctant to include them in the search for a solution. I was able in various meetings to dissipate these impressions, and relations improved significantly. I agreed with President Zinawi on a two-stage operation. The first stage, carried out in November and December 1992, was to plan for a series of bilateral discussions between the different leaders, in the presence of the elders, to map out the strategy for the conference itself. The conference would then be attended by a larger group of representatives from all the regions, the representatives being chosen by the local communities and not tutored by the faction leaders. This plan was also supported by the secretary-general of the OAU, Salim Ahmed Salim, and the secretary-general of the League of Arab States, Esmat Abdel Magid.

Meanwhile, the UNOSOM team had proposed to divide Somalia into four zones to encourage decentralization of all operations. The four zones would include Bossaso, Berbera, Kismayu, and Mogadishu. This decentralization would have made both UNOSOM and relief agencies less dependent on the conditions prevailing in Mogadishu and promoted the new regional leadership so badly needed by Somalia. This proposal was endorsed by the Security Council in Resolution 767 (see appendix B for the text of the resolution).

Here is how I assessed the situation at the donors' conference convened in Geneva on October 12, 1992:

1. Only two months ago, we succeeded in penetrating the interior remote areas of Somalia thanks to the airlift operation. Until then, the true depth of the humanitarian catastrophe was only partly perceived. Although

full access to all affected areas has not yet been achieved the available statistics and the horrific images seen so far on television screens across the globe have captured to a large extent the depth of this human tragedy. We know that it is a crisis of frightening proportions and that we are paying the price for past neglect. A whole year slipped whilst the United Nations and the international community, save for the ICRC and a few NGOs, watched Somalia descend into this hell.

2. The damage will not be repaired. I believe a minimum of 300,000 Somalis, mostly children, would have succumbed, some of them in agony, over the last year and a half. It should be a duty of the United Nations to look back and seriously investigate the reasons for our failure to act promptly. Because the important question is how we can in the future avert similar tragedies and improve the United Nations' preventive action, both political and humanitarian.

3. What picture can I give you of Somalia today? It is still a country without central, regional or local administrations and without any public utility services, no electricity, no communications, no health services, no schools. Potable water is scarce and the productive base, both urban and rural, has been almost completely destroyed. Anarchy prevails. The country and its cities are divided into pockets controlled by fractured political movements, factions and subclans. In the Northwest, one of the political movements has unilaterally proclaimed an independent "Republic of Somaliland." The southern part of Somalia remains unstable with a tenuous stalemate among the warlords who have battled for the control of various towns and villages. The tension in that area has been aggravated by disturbing incidents along the border. Hundreds of thousands of refugees are going back and forth seeking help with sometimes a flow of arms accompanying these cross-border movements.

4. Amid this chaos, however, some positive trends are beginning to emerge. The cease-fire agreements negotiated by the United Nations among the various warring factions in different regions have been respected to a great extent. Thus, since April–May, Somalia has not had large-scale fighting or major open hostilities of the kind we are currently witnessing in the former Yugoslavia. We have tried to move quickly to reinforce these positive trends. In Mogadishu, which was the epicentre of the heaviest fighting, fifty United Nations military observers were deployed last August and have contributed to some stabilization of the situation. They could do much better if they received the required logistical support. Two of them have been wounded in an ambush. I would like to pay tribute to their courage. It is not easy to move around and check on armed Somalis, while they are themselves unarmed.

5. Security remains a major problem. Lawlessness, banditry and looting have taken the place of major fighting and open factional hostilities.

Marauding armed groups, loyal to no particular warlord, but only to themselves, pose a grave threat to the safety of international personnel as well as the local population, and hinder the effective delivery and distribution of humanitarian supplies.

6. In order to address this security problem, five hundred United Nations security personnel are being deployed in Mogadishu. They will, in principle, ensure the protection of relief operations at the seaport and airport as well as along the routes used for the distribution of humanitarian assistance. This will, hopefully, contain looting and see to it that food reaches the areas where it is needed. The faction leaders in the Northeast have also signed an agreement for the deployment of 750 United Nations troops to provide security at the port of Bossaso and to ensure the effective delivery of humanitarian and rehabilitation assistance to the whole of that region. Negotiations are currently under way with the political leaders in the so-called "Somaliland" for the deployment of United Nations security personnel at the port of Berbera, and also with the leaders in the South for the same operation at the port of Kismayu, which has changed hands many times and presented us with serious security problems. The port of Kismayu is so important for emergency relief in the South that any delay in ensuring security there is to be strongly denounced. It should have had, with Mogadishu, our priority concern from the beginning.

7. There is, however, one related matter to which I must invite your attention. Owing to the complexity and sensitivity of the political and military situation in Somalia, it would not be possible for the United Nations security personnel to function effectively without the cooperation and support of some local Somali security arrangements. The most careful consideration has been given to this matter. The option of a national police force was explored but on reflection it was decided that such a police force, in the absence of national reconciliation, would present serious problems. Nor can we continue to rely on the services of the present so-called "technicals." We have, therefore, decided to establish a small security force of Somalis to assist United Nations forces at the airport, seaport, and the distribution centers, starting with Mogadishu where the United Nations troops have already arrived. It is only an arrangement of this nature that can assure safety for relief workers and protection for humanitarian supplies. This could ultimately form the nucleus of a Somali police country wide.

8. These proposed Somali guards would require uniforms, transport and communications equipment. It is an area where we need urgently the support and assistance of governments. I am pleased to note that some, like the French government, have already made some initial offers, but more of such assistance is required, urgently. These security conditions

Officials from the World Food Program and UNOSOM greet the first ship carrying UN emergency relief to enter the port of Mogadishu, May 1992.

Mohammed Farah Aideed (with hat) and a group of his supporters gather for a meeting with Mohamed Sahnoun near Bardera, summer 1992.

Mohamed Sahnoun meets with Somali journalists at UNOSOM headquarters in Mogadishu, summer 1992.

Somali leader Ali Mahdi, Mohamed Sahnoun, and Bernard Kouchner, French minister of health and humanitarian affairs (left to right), discuss the emergency relief operation in the northern part of Mogadishu, August 1992.

are an imperative today because the temptations for loot and greed are spreading with the prospect of more supplies reaching Somalia.

9. I am grateful to the entire donor community for the massive operations that have been launched in the past two months. Relief efforts have increased significantly since August. Thanks to more frequent shipments into the ports of Mogadishu and Kismayu, and to the airlift operation that started over this period, the relief community has been able to improve largely on its response to the needs of the Somali population. The British Government has informed us of a new large contribution and I know from press releases that other Governments have taken the same step. Thanks to this support from your Governments ICRC, WFP and UNICEF are providing now increased amounts of food and supplementary feeding supplies to the South of Somalia reaching an average of 20,000 MT a month. This is more than double the quantity supplied before the month of August. It remains far below the estimated minimum need of 50,000 MT.

10. In early August, France provided a direct shipment of 2,000 MT of food items and diesel fuel. Saudi Arabia sent 4,000 MT and another vessel is at present waiting to be unloaded at Mogadishu port. The Nigerian Government donated 2,000 MT of baby food which are currently being discharged by WFP in Mogadishu.

11. Now that shipments are being delivered on a more substantial and regular basis, our primary objective is to reach populations in an increasing number of villages and towns so as to stem the flow of displaced people, and prevent the creation of more "death camps" such as Baidoa.

12. Although belated, the airlifts and airdrops have clearly facilitated a much better penetration of the interior of Somalia, and have been a real, though tragic, eye-opener. Since the operation started, we have been able to increase gradually the capacity of each rotation. At present, this operation brings 240 MT per day to Mogadishu, Baidoa, Bardera, Wajit, Saco Uen and Belet Uen. The recent trial airdrop operation of a total of 150 tonnes to Tigielglo and El Garas has proved a success. It encountered no serious security problems and the recovery rate was estimated at 95 percent. These airdrops should certainly continue and expand because they help stop a further displacement of people.

13. Let me underline once more the fact that the airlift has made a tremendous difference in our response to the immediate needs of the starving population. Thousands of lives are being saved. The contributions of the U.S. Air Force, the German Air Force and the Royal Canadian Air Force have been crucial. Without the combined airlifts of these donors, likewise the French and Belgian donors, the provision of food assistance into isolated areas would have been practically

impossible. The airlift operation, if sustained, will allow us to explore all areas where access on the ground is still too difficult or too dangerous. I do appeal to these governments, while conveying to them the gratitude of so many Somalis, to please continue their magnificent efforts and sustain them for a while.

14. On the non-food side, WHO and UNICEF continue to provide drugs and essential medical supplies to Somalia but it is still insufficient as noticed by some of the distinguished visitors. The French Government is planning to establish a central pharmacy, initially in Djibouti. This is going to be extensively helpful, because more people are dying now of diseases including hunger-related diseases and the proportion of adult victims is higher; more than 50 percent. NGOs are strengthening their curative programmes and together with UNICEF are expanding their programmes of immunization and vaccination. Many NGOs are also promoting the establishment of therapeutic feeding centres both in central and southern Somalia.

15. OXFAM, which was engaged in agricultural assessments, has now committed itself to establishing a joint programme with UNICEF to provide seeds and tool provision. The programme will benefit up to 16,000 severely marginalized farming families in the Juba valley. WFP and ICRC will be providing the necessary food support to these families. This is the first significant integrated rehabilitation project undertaken in this region for over 18 months. Some other NGOs are planning to carry out a seeds and food distribution programme, and I believe this should be encouraged and supported by the donor countries. It is time we think also in terms of rehabilitation of the economic structure which many Somalis are pressing for.

16. The United Nations Development Programme is embarking on a comprehensive programme which involves this kind of rural rehabilitation as well as basic infrastructure, institutional building, and human development. Specifically, the agency is enhancing its current project for the restoration of water supply in Mogadishu and other towns. It is also planning to provide assistance in the area of air traffic control, reconstruction of power plants and distribution lines, as well as special public works programmes, with a large number of national professionals to be enrolled in these programmes.

17. The expansion of the emergency relief and rehabilitation has called for an increase in the number of relief workers operating on the ground. Both the United Nations agencies and non-governmental organizations have increased their staff significantly over the past two months. I cannot offer great enough praise to the large number of NGOs which have either started new specific projects in Somalia or given their valuable resources to existing operations. What a beautiful testimony

to human solidarity. Mobilization of local workers is also on the increase, following the objective of helping populations become self-sufficient as soon as possible.

18. One important area where many respectable elders have repeatedly asked for assistance is the disarmament of the population and the demobilization of irregular forces. The Somali nation has become hostage to gunmen. To rescue it from this predicament, we need to move as fast as possible to *create a responsible civil society. For this, a trust fund is needed.* With such a fund, we can endeavor to encourage the formation and activities of organizations with a vested interest in peace, such as elders' councils, youth movements, women's organizations, intellectual associations, professional associations and merchants' unions. Today, there are too many elements with a vested interest in disorder. They scorn peace.

19. I have been talking to many Somali intellectuals who are ready to assist in the rebuilding of their country. With the closure of all factories and institutes, and the collapse of Government departments, many qualified cadres in different fields remain unemployed. Their services could be utilized in the promotion of a responsible civil society while mapping out a recovery programme for the country. Similarly, they are ready to participate in the reactivation of the different vocational training centres which would offer venues for the absorption of Somali youth currently living by the gun, in the absence of other viable options. This is a better incentive than the food for arms swap which is currently having little success.

20. In all fairness, it would be less than truthful if I did not also refer to the problems of coordination that we are facing in our operations on the ground in Somalia. In order to facilitate the effective delivery and distribution of humanitarian assistance, and because of the total absence of local structures, the United Nations and all relief agencies have had to establish collaborative relationships on an ad hoc basis with some Somali partners. These include the so-called "technicals" for security, Somali ports and airports' self-appointed authorities, porters, transporters, drivers, landlords, merchants, Somali NGOs, and joint relief committees. United Nations agencies and NGOs have been negotiating separately with them regarding conditions of work, fees, tariffs, etc. This has led to escalated demands from the Somalis, and contributed to security problems in cases where armed "technicals" and guards have used, or threatened to use, force to have their demands met. We are currently going through a period of transition after which a system will be developed to ensure coordination and equity in conducting business with our Somali partners. I appeal for the cooperation of all, especially on the part of big agencies.

21. Moreover, in dealing with the representatives of the various Somali parties, factions and movements, some agency field officers furnish these leaders with information that conflicts with the reports they make to us. This has often resulted in serious political problems. It represents a great liability in organizing our operations in Somalia. Unless it is redressed, the effectiveness of our efforts and programmes will be enormously undermined.

22. We have also faced problems from the lack of coordination regarding the arrival of vessels carrying humanitarian supplies at Somali ports. While we welcome all relief vessels, those that come unannounced are the cause of serious concern for us. Some ships have had to stay offshore for several days awaiting arrangements for security, unloading, negotiations for payment of port tariffs and unloading fees, and arrangements for storage or transportation. I wish to appeal to all concerned to consult with us so that vessels will leave for Somalia with a clear understanding of how their cargo is to be handled upon arrival. It is also clear that the security situation might compel us to delay the movement of ships; and we, therefore, need the total cooperation and understanding of all.

23. I should also mention that the quality of foodstuffs delivered to Somalia matters a great deal. High quality items such as sugar, rice, flour, and cooking oil, while very much welcome, have many times caused unnecessary deaths and injury because, by and large, they invite looting and consequent fighting. Our experience has shown that for grains, looting is estimated at 15% of delivered supplies, while for high quality items, the percentage can be as high as 40%. It has been disheartening for me to visit hospitals and to see wounded people smeared with the very flour that is supposed to save their lives. It is, therefore, very important for donor countries to consult with us on the types, quality and priority destination of items that could be sent to Somalia. As the people on the spot, we are in a position to offer advice on this and where food items could be delivered.

24. I would, in this connection, very strongly recommend that the issue of monetization be seriously taken up. There is so much hesitation and lack of motivation when I bring up the subject that I now despair of seeing this very important operation ever implemented. Yet in my discussions with Somalis, I find a total adherence to this notion which everybody agrees will enable us to resolve many crucial problems and enhance security. It will provide jobs to Somalis and involve them more in the process of reestablishing market activities throughout the country.

25. Let me make a special plea for the Northwest, the Northeast and Central Somalia. There is no greater need for the restitution of war

damage than in the Northwest (Somaliland), which has also been shamefully neglected. Somaliland's two major cities, Hargeisa and Burao, and several of its smaller towns and villages, were almost totally devastated by a combination of air bombardment, ground missiles and other heavy weapons during the last years of Siad Barre's tenure. Without electricity and running water, with thousands of uninhabitable dwellings and land mines numbering tens of thousands, the region's plight cries out for new concentrated efforts towards rehabilitation. Whilst the needs of starving populations in Southern Somalia have captured world attention, understandably, Somaliland, the Northeastern and the Central region, must no longer be neglected. They must receive an equitable share of humanitarian assistance and help with reconstruction. In fact, the Northeast, because of its relative stability and good cooperation with the United Nations, can become a model for the other regions and deserves a special attention aiming at a comprehensive recovery programme. It might be a key to an overall solution of the Somali problem.

26. The delivery of relief assistance and the security arrangements that we are putting into place will not by themselves resolve the crisis in Somalia. They are mere stopgap measures. The solution lies in the achievement of national reconciliation among all the Somali parties, factions and movements which could lead to the restoration of Government and a return to normalcy. Without national reconciliation to facilitate reconstruction and the restoration of economic activity, Somalia will become a bottomless pit into which the donor community will continue to pour humanitarian assistance with no end in sight. And, thus, the risk of renewal of hostilities will continue to haunt us. Therefore, we need to convene a national reconciliation conference as soon as possible. We have been undertaking intensive consultations in this regard with the Somali political leaders and elders both at the regional and national level. I am glad to say that we are making considerable progress. We hope at the end of the year, all the parties, movements and factions will participate in a national reconciliation conference. There are now real possibilities of crossing the threshold into a phase where all factions will be engaged in dialogue. But there remain a few hurdles we need to overcome. These hurdles are not insurmountable. We need the support of all Governments. There are some Governments with greater influence and leverage on some of the parties, and with their support and assistance, the process of national reconciliation could begin very soon. I wish to avail myself of this opportunity to express my gratitude to the leaders of the Horn of Africa and other Governments that have given their political support to my efforts to establish a dialogue among the Somali parties.

27. In conclusion, I wish to inform you that the United Nations is now strengthening its presence in Somalia. We are opening zonal political offices in Mogadishu, Bossaso, Hargeisa and Kismayu. These offices will be responsible for promoting reconciliation at the regional levels, negotiating with the local leaders in order to remove any impediments to the effective delivery of humanitarian assistance, liaising with other relief agencies operating in these areas and promoting rehabilitation and effective administrations. I would like to encourage governmental and intergovernmental agencies to start now returning to Somalia and joining in the efforts to begin the reconstruction process.

Unfortunately, several serious problems created by wrong and unjustified moves of the UN management, both at headquarters and by some agencies' representatives in the field, continued to hamper our efforts.

First, despite significant contributions made by donor countries through increased shipment and airlift deliveries of humanitarian assistance, most UN agencies were not able to fulfill their pledges and organize a massive emergency relief operation as was done in Ethiopia in the early '80s or even in Biafra in the late '60s. I stressed this point again in the meeting held by the donor countries and agencies in Geneva on October 12 in New York and in my discussion with the UN secretary-general, who clearly expressed his support and who promised to write personally to the heads of agencies.[56]

Second, the UN agencies would hardly leave Mogadishu, Nairobi, and Djibouti, and the tendency to centralize everything in Mogadishu became a feature of UNOSOM operations. I received practically no response to my numerous requests to the agencies to fill the posts and responsibilities allocated to them in the four zones the Security Council had designated. Delivery of emergency relief and rehabilitation operations continued to be concentrated in Mogadishu, giving Aideed and his allies a certain leverage. This centralization also undermined UNOSOM's efforts to organize grassroots structures in local communities within the regions.

Third, most agencies were reluctant to seriously coordinate their activities with UNOSOM, which would have helped enhance the security measures we envisaged. We proposed to use monetization of a reasonable percentage of the food delivery to encourage cooperation from the local merchants. These merchants were prepared to use their influence to check the activities of the armed looters and the mischief of some of the militia leaders. I had several meetings with these merchants, who complained that the agencies were allowing much of the food brought in to be marketed by guards, looters, and other "agents," thus undermining their attempt to build up a sound market. It is clear that ultimately these merchants had to make some deals with the looters, which encouraged the looters to increase their harassment of the relief work. Exasperated by the slow response of the UN, the U.S. government offered a plan to deliver food to the Somali people, using both assistance and commercial channels. The United States proposed to distribute approximately 70,000 tons of free food to the destitute and to sell another 70,000 tons cheaply to vendors in the hope that this measure would lower overall food prices and increase food availability.[57]

I also proposed that the agencies harmonize their payment rates for services and the use of facilities and that they take a number of other steps that would have greatly limited the ability of the militia and the looters to affect our operations. But most agencies' representatives seemed to resent any authority except their own headquarters', and coordination became an impossible task.[58] Although looting was limited in October 1992 to 10 percent of the delivery, according to the ICRC (15 percent according to the WFP), it could have been reduced further if these steps had been taken.

Fourth, the bureaucratic approach of the UN headquarters in New York tended to ignore UNOSOM's advice and warnings in sensitive matters related to security. It was time-consuming and difficult for the UNOSOM team to negotiate the Somali leaders' agreement for the deployment of 500 UN troops for the security of humanitarian assistance, and we were hoping the troops would be deployed right away. There is no doubt that, had these 500 troops been fully deployed as late as a month after the agreement, that is, at the beginning of September, it would have made an appreciable difference in the environment. Somali leaders, NGOs, UN agencies, and especially the people of Mogadishu were eagerly waiting for these troops to appear. The UN had already deployed fifty unarmed military observers in Mogadishu, and they were doing excellent work far beyond their mandate, even to the point of getting involved in peacemaking between different militias and escorting relief convoys from the port to the northern part of Mogadishu.[59] The bureaucratic delays and the skirmishes at headquarters between different departments led to total confusion as to priorities. The 500 troops expected had not even arrived when an announcement was made in New York that more than 3,000 troops would be sent to Somalia. This statement was made without informing the UNOSOM delegation in Mogadishu or the leaders of the neighboring countries, who had previously been informed by me of every intended move. Worse, the announcement was made without consulting the Somali leaders and community elders.[60]

Fifth, as the UN began to gain the trust of the warring parties and acceptance and sympathy among the people, the UNOSOM team in Mogadishu learned that a Russian plane with UN markings and chartered by a UN agency had delivered currency and military equipment to the north of Mogadishu, apparently to the troops supporting interim president Ali Mahdi. This, of course, infuriated his arch-rival Aideed. Suspicion of all UN personnel was spreading in Mogadishu. The Russian plane's delivery rekindled the old perception of many Somalis that the UN and some countries were biased in favor of Ali Mahdi. There was some confusion as to whether the plane was still under lease to the UN agency concerned, that is, the World Food Program. The UN Office of Legal Affairs concluded that the lease contract remained in force at the time of the flight. The agencies concerned were unable to explain how their representatives had lost track of the plane and how a relatively big operation such as a shipment of currency and military equipment could have gone unnoticed. The UN Office of Legal Affairs suggested that an investigation be carried out in Nairobi. Such an investigation would show the good faith of the UN to all concerned, including the Somali population and the governments of the neighboring countries, especially because there were rumors and indications that more than one such flight had taken place. In fact, late in October another Russian plane, also carrying suspicious cargo, crashed in northern Mogadishu on an illegal flight. These flights might well have been in clear contradiction to resolution 733 of January 23, 1992, which imposed a "general and complete embargo on all deliveries of weapons and military equipment to Somalia." What is incredible is that although the UN's name and reputation were at stake, no serious investigation was undertaken and no legal action for redress was pursued.

Furthermore, although after learning of these incidents we had issued a statement addressed to the UN agencies concerned advising strongly against their continued use of those companies and brokerage firms involved in the incidents, we were shocked to see some important UN personalities landing in Somalia on the same Antonov planes. These arrivals further fueled the rumors about UN bias and even corruption.

These are only a few examples of the organizational obstacles UNOSOM encountered while attempting to address the issues of starvation and civil war in Somalia. My hope was that with the personal support of the UN secretary-general I could ultimately tackle these difficulties and gradually create an environment for serious peace talks, not so much between the faction leaders as between new leaders being promoted by the grassroots process. UNOSOM had already succeeded in putting together, with the help of the Swedish Institute of Life and Peace, a conference of Somali intellectuals representing the four zones designated by the UN Security Council. At the end of October 1992, two small planes brought these outstanding intellectuals out of Somalia into the Seychelles, where, despite the usual suspicion and animosity between clans, they eventually sat together and produced some excellent suggestions on how to resolve the pressing issues of national reconciliation and initiate the reconstruction of the country.

While I was holding these meetings I received two surprising messages from the secretary-general: the first questioning my presence in the Seychelles and the second ordering me to refrain from any criticism of the UN agencies. It was more than one could tolerate from the UN bureaucracy that had inspired such criticism. I offered my resignation from the position of special representative and proposed to continue my mission as a special envoy of the secretary-general, working under his authority and responsible only to him. This proposal was not accepted, and I issued the following statement at a press conference on October 29, 1992:

> Following my resignation as the Special Representative of the Secretary-General of the United Nations for Somalia on 26 October 1992, I have been overwhelmed by appeals from all sections of Somali society, foreign governments, non-governmental organizations, and United Nations officials to reconsider my decision. I feel duty-bound to all my friends, who have expressed concern about my resignation, to state that it was no wish

of mine to leave Somalia and all the wonderful people who have given, and continue to give, at great risk to themselves, their time and energy to save the lives of the starving populations of Somalia.

For this reason, and despite bitter experiences with the UN bureaucracy, I proposed to the Secretary-General in my letter of resignation that I would be prepared, if he so wished, to assume at any time the function of temporary Special Envoy in order to address some specific, urgent problems in Somalia. I have received no response to my letter of 26 October.

I would like to express my appreciation for the unswerving support and encouragement I have received, even up to the last moment, from all quarters of Somali society, all relief workers, and various governments, during the last six months that I have had the honour of undertaking this mission.

I am gratified by the progress that has been made during this period—from very low levels of humanitarian assistance to the stage we have now reached when serious assistance, in large quantities, is now being delivered by sea, road and air. Political progress towards reconciliation has also, I am pleased to report, shown marked improvement during the last few weeks. I am greatly encouraged and wish all Somalis happier times ahead.

4 The Issue of Intervention versus Sovereignty

*A*MONG THE reasons that inhibit the world community and the UN from intervening in conflicts within states is the principle of sovereignty. Failure to intervene earlier in conflicts such as that in Somalia, even by providing mediation and good offices and for the purpose of stemming human tragedy, has been justified on the grounds that the international community has no right to interfere in the internal affairs of sovereign states. In this context two questions need to be asked: First, what is sovereignty? Second, how is sovereignty really related to the prohibition of political and humanitarian intervention?

On the issue of sovereignty, Alan James has noted that "when states refer to themselves as sovereign they mean that they are all, in terms of their individual constitutional schemes, independent of any larger units of a like kind."[61] Capacity for international activity and the acceptance by other states of the legitimacy of this activity is another characteristic of sovereignty.[62] In this formulation, there should be no doubt that all states share equal status. However, the condition of sovereignty leads states to be bound by customary international laws and rules. It should be noted that the prohibition against interference in the internal affairs of states has arisen from international law but is not concomitant with sovereignty. In other words, as James notes, "The right to run its own affairs stems from a state's individual constitutional set-up. The duty not to intervene in another state stems from international law. The former could exist without the latter, leaving calculations and comments about intervention exclusively to the *political plane*."[63] It is in the UN Charter and in the General

Assembly resolutions as well as in the decisions of the various regional organizations that the "political plane" is determined.

Article 2 of the UN Charter states, "The organization is based on the principle of the sovereign equality of all its members." It states further, "Nothing in the Charter shall authorize the United Nations to intervene in matters which are essentially within the domestic jurisdiction of any state." However, exceptions to this rule are built into the charter, which states that this principle (the principle of nonintervention) shall not prejudice the application of enforcement measures under Chapter VII. Member states of the UN are also reminded that they have international obligations: "All members shall fulfill in good faith the obligations assumed by them in accordance with the Charter." These obligations are spelled out within the purposes of the UN, which are "to bring about by peaceful means, and in conformity with the principles of justice and international law, adjustment or settlement of international disputes or situations which might lead to a breach of the peace" and "to achieve international cooperation in solving international problems of economic, social, cultural or humanitarian character, and in promoting and encouraging respect for human rights and fundamental freedoms for all without distinction of race, sex, language, or religion" (Article 1).

Finally, Article 34 stipulates that "the Security Council may investigate any dispute, or any situation which might lead to international friction or give rise to a dispute, in order to determine whether the continuance of the dispute or situation is likely to endanger the maintenance of international peace and security."

The use of the word *situation* in Article 1 and Article 34, together with the enforcement powers of Chapter VII, opens up the charter to a broader reading than the one usually given. The framers of the charter, in their wisdom, clearly referred to situations that might lead to a breach of the peace in addition to disputes. Although they did not qualify further what they meant by *situation*, it seems clear that they were thinking of some internal situations that can have a direct bearing on international relations and can cause tensions leading to a larger conflict. They must have had in mind how an internal situation in Austria brought about the *Anschluss* or how the role of minorities, including German minorities in Czechoslovakia, Poland, and Hungary, affected the situation in Europe and led finally to the Second World War. So the word *situation* in Article 1 and Article 34 provides an important clue as to the concern of the drafters of the charter and how in their view any situation in internal or interstate conflicts that could lead to a larger regional or international war may be investigated by the UN.

After the drafting of the charter, the international community expressed its support for the right of humanitarian assistance through the adoption of the Universal Declaration of Human Rights in 1948 and the four Geneva conventions in 1949. So the charter, the declaration, and the Geneva conventions, as well as the UN Convention for the Prevention and Punishment of Genocide and the 1951 Convention on Refugees and their protocols, should be taken together to better understand the meaning of "interventions" as intended by the framers of the charter. More than any Security Council resolution, this initial, comprehensive, and fully persuasive body of international legislation gives the right and obligation to both the UN and regional organizations to come to the rescue of endangered populations by providing relief and actively contributing to the resolution of the conflict itself.

As charters are constitutional documents, it is the duty of statesmen to undertake to interpret them in the light of developments in international law.

David Scheffer, in his essay on humanitarian intervention versus state sovereignty, outlines five categories of exceptions to the Article 2(7) prohibitions against interference in states' internal affairs:

- First, the obvious exception is a Chapter VII enforcement action as stated in Article 2(7) itself.
- A second exception to Article 2(7) is international treaty commitments. These commitments include, for example, the many international and regional human rights treaties, including the Convention against Genocide.
- A third exception is the presence of anarchy or the absence of consensual authority.
- A fourth exception exists when consent to intervene would be required from an illegitimate government.
- The fifth and probably most important exception is in the case of systematic violation of the human rights of large groups of people within borders. This condition has been repeatedly articulated as an exception to Article 2(7).[64]

Actually, the above categories underline the fact that much of the discussion of humanitarian and political intervention revolves not so much around the principle of intervention as such, but around the issue of consent. In the past, the government of a state had to consent to humanitarian intervention or it could not be undertaken. Of late, the international community has had to begin to act in cases where the host government is unwilling to allow humanitarian intervention or unable to authorize intervention. This latest development will gradually make it difficult for governments to refuse their consent in specific circumstances to an intervention that would primarily provide their people with humanitarian assistance and political good offices. International pressure might become so overwhelming that any objection would find little support from any credible quarter. It should be clear, however, that to be credible and successful the intervention must be based on a consensus and must be perceived as a normal, legal, and moral move on the part of the international community that does not have to take on the character of a forced armed intervention. Such an intervention should indeed first go through the different phases of a preventive policy program. And if security forces are ultimately needed to protect relief efforts, to monitor the cessation of hostilities, and to keep the peace, they should strictly serve those objectives and not interfere otherwise in the domestic affairs of the country.

The preventive policy program should make full use of regional arrangements, as the UN Charter, Article 33, clearly states. At one stage or another, especially if the use of force is envisaged, the contribution of the UN General Assembly to the decision-making process is also advisable. The assembly's participation will remove any suspicion as to the legitimacy of an intervention and emphasize the fact that this intervention does not necessarily imply any legal limitation of the principle of sovereignty. A debate in the General Assembly might delay action, but it would leave no doubt as to the common resolve of the international community to deal seriously with a specific conflict without jeopardizing some fundamental principles of international law. The General Assembly itself can, according to the charter, make recommendations by a two-thirds majority with respect to the maintenance of international peace and security.

In addition, a debate in the General Assembly will make it clear that not only governments but also regional organizations, spiritual leaders, and humanitarian institutions feel a moral duty to show their concern for the suffering of large segments of populations anywhere. When human rights are purely and simply ignored or systematically suppressed; when a ruling group, military or civilian, oppresses a whole population; when tragic and endless confrontation occurs within a society on a religious, tribal, ethnic, or political basis; when the whole state is breaking down— with whom does sovereignty ultimately reside?

What is really required at an early stage is the availability of resources for mediation or conciliation and, if necessary, for humanitarian or peacekeeping intervention. Such resources should be available first at the regional level, and if regional efforts produce little or no result, the matter should then be addressed by the appropriate structures of the UN. Where the ingredients of a serious crisis are already present, the international community should act and act quickly. The concerns about forcible intervention, the use of military force, and the expenses and the risks involved would be less inhibiting if this availability, in both humanitarian and political fields, were demonstrated and translated into action as soon as possible, as required in Article 33 of the UN Charter. Intervention would not have to conflict with the principle of sovereignty. The issue is *prevention*, which could be achieved through an early diagnosis of the situation followed by mediation, conciliation, arbitration, and assistance with pressuring the parties concerned.

Former Secretary-General Javier Pérez de Cuéllar noted with respect to Article 2(7), "One could—and I would even say, should—inquire whether certain other texts that were later adopted by the United Nations, in particular the Universal Declaration of Human Rights, do not implicitly call into question this inviolable notion of sovereignty."[65]

In *An Agenda for Peace*, Secretary-General Boutros Boutros-Ghali stated:

The foundation stone of the work is and must remain the State. Respect for its fundamental sovereignty and integrity are crucial to any common international progress. The time of absolute and exclusive sovereignty, however, has passed; its theory was never matched by reality. It is the task of leaders of states to understand this and to find a balance between the needs of good internal governance and the requirements of an ever more interdependent world.[66]

OAU Secretary-General Salim Ahmed Salim, while not questioning the importance of national sovereignty, stated, "Nobody can suggest to me that we can invoke sovereignty and argue against a collective decision to put an end to the misery, anarchy, chaos, and mayhem that, for example, is taking place in Somalia."[67] In Salim's view, sovereignty could be used to empower the OAU and the African states to pool their resources for a greater good.

5 Conclusion

*T*HE SECRETARY-GENERAL'S untimely announcement, made without proper consultation, that the UN would send in additional reinforcements, followed by my resignation as special representative, led to a rapid deterioration of the security situation in Mogadishu and elsewhere. Armed groups of Somalis began to harass the relief efforts more actively. Although the ninety-day plan of April 1992 had given way to the one-hundred-day plan for accelerated relief deliveries approved on October 12, 1992, a UN report on the plan dated December 3, 1992, stated, "Some 38 days into the Programme, it is clear that while much has been accomplished, even the short-term needs are not being met."[68] Of a target amount of 100,000 MT of food supplies, between October 12 and December 3 the World Food Program delivered only 18,900 MT.[69] Shortfalls in assistance continued to be manifested and the security situation deteriorated markedly.[70] Estimates of the amount of food being stolen ranged now from 10 percent to 80 percent. The U.S. government used the higher figure as part of the justification for Operation Restore Hope.[71]

On November 24, 1992, the secretary-general sent a letter to the Security Council outlining five options for Somalia. The first option was to deploy the 2,400 troops authorized by Security Council Resolution 775. The secretary-general decided that the situation in Somalia had deteriorated past the "point at which it is susceptible to the peace-keeping treatment."[72] The second option, which the secretary-general rejected, was to withdraw the military elements of UNOSOM. The third option was a show of force in Mogadishu by the UN. The obstacles to this option were obvious, as the Somali warlords possessed significant quantities of both light and heavy weapons. A fourth option was to have the member states undertake a nationwide enforcement operation. The operation would be authorized by the Security Council. Acting American Secretary of State Lawrence Eagleburger stated that the United States would be willing to spearhead such an operation. The fifth option was a countrywide enforcement operation with UN, as opposed to member state, command and control. The secretary-general acknowledged that the UN did not have the capability to command and control an operation of the size required.[73] This statement was a clear indication of the secretary-general's preference. On December 3, 1992, the UN Security Council adopted Resolution 794, which authorized member states to use all possible means to establish a secure environment for humanitarian relief. American troops landed in Somalia on December 9, 1992.

What is the lesson of all of this? It is high time to look closely at the overall management of UN activities, at headquarters and in the field. For several years now, there have been calls for reform of the UN system, and a number of recommendations have been made and studies undertaken. But so far little progress has been made in improving the efficiency of the organization and preparing it for the challenges it is facing even now.

The legacy of the Cold War is being felt both in the ineptitude of the UN's structures and in the waste of its human resources. The existing structures are not at all adapted to the requirements of the new era, especially in apprehending the whole problem of conflict both between and within states. During the Cold War era, there was a tendency to establish committees and departments for all kinds of purposes. Some of these units were created simply to avoid further discussion of an issue or to satisfy the demands of particular delegations. Very often members of these delegations later became staff members of the very committees or departments they helped to create. In fact, much of the recruitment of UN staff is done through governments and embassies, and the recruitment process does not necessarily respect the criteria of competence and experience. Even less regard is given the criterion of commitment. Article 101(3) of the UN Charter states, "The paramount consideration in the employment of the staff and in the determination of the conditions of service shall be the necessity of securing the highest standards of efficiency, competence, and integrity. Due regard shall be paid to the importance of recruiting the staff on as wide a geographical basis as possible." The fact is, however, that today the UN's obsolete structures are draining its resources, both human and material. The UN will not be able to perform its vital functions if it does not make better use of its existing resources. The organization's bureaucracy has to be streamlined so that all opportunities for preconflict intervention can be thoroughly exploited. What the UN needs today is a greater focus on early warning mechanisms.

The UN headquarters must establish strong permanent and functional relationships with the regional organizations so that they can coordinate their response to specific needs in different regions of the world. The current system is not adapted to the post–Cold War international environment and routinely reacts to crisis through improvisation. This explains why there are so many delays and contradictions in the UN's response to crisis, for instance, its incapacity to respond earlier to the crisis in Somalia, or the incredible confusion connected with the transportation of the 500 security personnel from Pakistan to Somalia and the problems surrounding their deployment. The affair of the Russian planes with UN markings that were involved in illegal flights with suspicious cargoes raises some important questions about the credibility and the neutrality of the UN agencies involved.

While there has been much discussion about the mandate of the UN and the different political organs as well as the so-called financial deficit, very little attention has been given to ethics, transparency, efficiency, control, and accountability. When reports are made by high officials looking into corruption or inefficiency, they are suppressed.[74] My own experience with the top levels of UN bureaucracy was terribly frustrating.

In principle, the Security Council and the General Assembly are supposed to monitor and control the activities of the Secretariat. In reality, monitoring and control are done only on the basis of reports submitted by the Secretariat. The Security Council and the General Assembly have hardly been able to question the methods used, as well as the approach and even sometimes the policy pursued by the secretary-general, for instance in his handling of the Somali issue when UNOSOM II took over from Operation Restore Hope. Thousands of Somalis were killed and more than eighty UN officers lost their lives. It is difficult to see how management can improve its performance in implementing the decisions of the Security Council and the General Assembly if there is no close scrutiny of its activities, no streamlining of its structures, and no rational use of its human resources.

The challenges of the post–Cold War era require the world community to develop effective instruments for peacemaking and peacekeeping in the broader sense, which means dealing with the root causes, from preventing conflicts to rebuilding war-torn societies and pursuing sustainable development policies globally. These instruments exist in the form of the UN and its agencies, such as the Bretton Woods institutions. The question is, how can we make them more effective?

The answer is clear—they should be managed in the same way the best institutions, both private and public, are managed. The Security Council and the General Committee of the General Assembly should develop a series of mechanisms and criteria through which they can control the activities of the UN at headquarters and in the field and make the players accountable. They should then make sure that they choose the best chief executive officer available. The selection of the secretary-general should not be accomplished according to the criteria and methods currently used—regional rotation, lobbying, national interest, and so forth. We might end up having a maverick at the top of the UN. The Security Council should go through a short list of the best statesmen, managers, and intellectuals in the world and choose on the basis of competence, experience, and above all, ethical and moral authority. In this way, the international community will be able to forge an instrument capable of addressing the burning issues of peace, sustainable development, and democracy.

Appendix A
Somali Clans and Political Parties

Somali society can be divided into two tribal groups: Samal and Sab. The larger Samal group includes the following clans: Hawiye, Darod, Issaq, and Dir. The Sab group includes the Digil and Rahanwein clans. All of these clans are themselves subdivided into several subclans and family groups.

Political movements were created fairly recently along the lines of the clan structures.

1. *United Somali Congress (USC).* The USC was created by the Hawiye clan in central Somalia around Mogadishu. It is, however, currently split into two factions, one led by Mohammed Farah Aideed and the other led by Ali Mahdi.

2. *Somali Salvation Democratic Front (SSDF).* The SSDF was created by the Majertain subclan of the Darod, who live in northeast Somalia.

3. *Somali National Front (SNF).* This is the movement of the Marehan subclan of the Darod, who live in southern Somalia on the Kenyan border. The former president of Somalia, Siad Barre, belongs to this subclan.

4. *Somali National Movement (SNM).* The SNM was created by the Issaq clan of northwestern Somalia. Since May 1991, the SNM has proclaimed the independence of Somaliland in this region.

5. *Somali Patriotic Front (SPF)*. The SPF was founded by the Ogadeni, a subclan of the Darod who live partly in southern and partly in central Somalia. It is currently split into two factions.

6. *Somali Democratic Movement (SDM)*. The SDM is the movement of the Rahanwein clan, most of whom are sedentary farmers who live in southern and western Somalia. This clan is also split into two factions.

7. *Somali Democratic Association (SDA)*. The SDA is the party of the Dir clan living in northwestern Somalia.

There are numerous smaller parties in Somalia, as well as coalitions of parties such as the Somali National Alliance (SNA), which is a group of pro-Aideed factions.

APPENDIX B
UN Security Council Resolutions on Somalia

Resolution 733
(adopted 23 January 1992 by unanimous vote)

The Security Council,

Considering the request by Somalia for the Security Council to consider the situation in Somalia (S/23445),

Having heard the report of the Secretary-General on the situation in Somalia and commending the initiative taken by him in the humanitarian field,

Gravely alarmed at the rapid deterioration of the situation in Somalia and the heavy loss of human life and widespread material damage resulting from the conflict in the country and aware of its consequences on the stability and peace in the region,

Concerned that the continuation of this situation constitutes, as stated in the report of the Secretary-General, a threat to international peace and security,

Recalling its primary responsibility under the Charter of the United Nations for the maintenance of international peace and security,

Recalling also the provisions of Chapter VIII of the Charter of the United Nations,

Expressing its appreciation to the international and regional organizations that have provided assistance to the populations affected by the conflict and deploring that personnel of these organizations have lost their lives in the exercise of their humanitarian tasks,

Taking note of the appeals addressed to the parties by the Chairman of the Organization of the Islamic Conference on 16 December 1991, the Secretary-General of the Organization of African Unity on 18 December 1991 (S/23469) and the League of Arab States on 5 January 1992 (S/23448),

1. Takes note of the report of the Secretary-General on the situation in Somalia and expresses its concerns with the situation prevailing in that country;

2. Requests that the Secretary-General immediately undertake the necessary actions to increase humanitarian assistance of the United Nations and its specialized agencies to the affected population in all parts of Somalia in liaison with the other international humanitarian organizations and to this end to appoint a coordinator to oversee the effective delivery of this assistance;

3. Requests the Secretary-General of the United Nations, in cooperation with the Secretary-General of the Organization of African Unity and the Secretary-General of the League of Arab States, immediately contact all parties involved in the conflict, to seek their commitment to the cessation of hostilities to permit the humanitarian assistance to be distributed, to promote a cease-fire and compliance therewith, and to assist in the process of a political settlement of the conflict in Somalia;

4. Strongly urges all parties to the conflict immediately to cease hostilities and agree to a cease-fire and to promote the process of reconciliation and of political settlement in Somalia;

5. Decides, under Chapter VII of the Charter of the United Nations, that all States shall, for the purposes of establishing peace and stability in Somalia immediately implement a general and complete embargo on all deliveries of weapons and military equipment to Somalia until the Security Council decides otherwise;

6. Calls on all States to refrain from any action which might contribute to increasing tension and to impeding or delaying a peaceful and negotiated outcome to the conflict in Somalia, which would permit all Somalis to decide upon and to construct their future in peace;

7. Calls upon all parties to cooperate with the Secretary-General to this end and to facilitate the delivery by the United Nations, its specialized agencies and other humanitarian organizations of humanitarian assistance to all those in need of it, under the supervision of the coordinator;

8. Urges all parties to take all the necessary measures to ensure the safety of personnel sent to provide humanitarian assistance, to assist them in their tasks and to ensure full respect for the rules and principles of international law regarding the protection of civilian populations;

9. Calls upon all States and international organizations to contribute to the efforts of humanitarian assistance to the population of Somalia;

10. Requests the Secretary-General to report to the Security Council as soon as possible on this matter;

11. Decides to remain seized of the matter until a peaceful solution is achieved.

Resolution 746
(adopted 17 March 1992 by unanimous vote)

The Security Council,

Considering the request by Somalia for the Security Council to consider the situation in Somalia (S/23445),

Reaffirming its resolution 733 (1992) of 23 January 1992,

Having considered the report of the Secretary-General on the situation in Somalia (S/23693),

Taking note of the signing of the cease-fire agreements in Mogadishu on 3 March 1992, including the agreements for the implementation of measures aimed at stabilizing the cease-fire through a United Nations monitoring mission,

Deeply regretting that the factions have not yet abided by their commitment to implement the cease-fire and thus have still not permitted the unimpeded provision and distribution of humanitarian assistance to the people in need in Somalia,

Deeply disturbed by the magnitude of human suffering caused by the conflict and concerned that the continuation of the situation in Somalia constitutes a threat to international peace and security,

Bearing in mind that the factors described in paragraph 76 of the Secretary-General's report (S/23693) must be taken into account,

Cognizant of the importance of cooperation between the United Nations and regional organizations in the context of Chapter VIII of the Charter of the United Nations,

Underlining the importance which it attaches to the international, regional and non-governmental organizations, including the International Committee of the Red Cross, continuing to provide humanitarian and other relief assistance to the people of Somalia under difficult circumstances,

Expressing its appreciation to the regional organizations, including the Organization of African Unity, the League of Arab States and the Organization of the Islamic Conference, for their cooperation with the United Nations in the effort to resolve the Somali problem,

1. Takes note with appreciation of the report of the Secretary-General;

2. Urges the Somali factions to honor their commitment under the cease-fire agreements of 3 March 1992;

3. Urges all the Somali factions to cooperate with the Secretary-General and to facilitate the delivery by the United Nations and its specialized agencies and other humanitarian organizations of humanitarian assistance to all those in need of it, under the supervision of the coordinator mentioned in resolution 733 (1992);

4. Requests the Secretary-General to pursue his humanitarian efforts in Somalia and to use all the resources at his disposal, including those of the relevant United Nations agencies, to address urgently the critical needs of the affected population in Somalia;

5. Appeals to all Member States and to all humanitarian organizations to contribute to and to cooperate with these humanitarian relief efforts;

6. Strongly supports the Secretary-General's decision urgently to dispatch a technical team to Somalia, accompanied by the coordinator, in order to work within the framework and objectives outlined in paragraphs 73 and 74 of his report (S/23693) and to submit expeditiously a report to the Security Council on this matter;

7. Requests that the technical team also develop a high priority plan to establish mechanisms to ensure the unimpeded delivery of humanitarian assistance;

8. Calls on all parties, movements and factions in Mogadishu in particular, and Somalia in general, to respect fully the security and safety of the technical team and the personnel of the humanitarian organizations and to guarantee their complete freedom of movement in and around Mogadishu and other parts of Somalia;

9. Calls upon the Secretary-General of the United Nations to continue, in close cooperation with the Organization of African Unity, the League

of Arab States and the Organization of the Islamic Conference, his consultations with all Somali parties, movements and factions towards the convening of a conference for national reconciliation and unity in Somalia;

10. Calls upon all Somali parties, movements and factions to cooperate fully with the Secretary-General in the implementation of this resolution;

11. Decides to remain seized of the matter until a peaceful resolution is achieved.

Resolution 751
(adopted 24 April 1992 by unanimous vote)

The Security Council,

Considering the request by Somalia for the Security Council to consider the situation in Somalia (S/23445),

Reaffirming its resolutions 733 (1992) of 23 January 1992 and 746 (1992) of 17 March 1992,

Having considered the report of the Secretary-General on the situation in Somalia (S/23829 and Add.1 and Add.2),

Taking note of the signing of the cease-fire agreements in Mogadishu on 3 March 1992, including the agreements for the implementation of measures aimed at stabilizing the cease-fire through a United Nations monitoring mission,

Taking note also of the signing of letters of agreement in Mogadishu, Hargeisa and Kismayu on the mechanism for monitoring the cease-fire and arrangements for the equitable and effective distribution of humanitarian assistance in and around Mogadishu,

Deeply disturbed by the magnitude of human suffering caused by the conflict and concerned that the continuation of the situation in Somalia constitutes a threat to international peace and security,

Cognizant of the importance of cooperation between the United Nations and regional organizations in the context of Chapter VIII of the Charter of the United Nations,

Underlining the importance which it attaches to the international, regional and non-governmental organizations, including the International Committee of the Red Cross, continuing to provide humanitarian and other relief assistance to the people of Somalia under difficult circumstances,

Expressing its appreciation to the regional organizations, including the Organization of African Unity, the League of Arab States and the Organization of the Islamic Conference, for their cooperation with the United Nations in the effort to resolve the Somali problem,

1. Takes note with appreciation of the report of the Secretary-General of 21 April 1992 (S/23829 and Add.1 and Add.2);

2. Decides to establish under its authority, and in support of the Secretary-General in accordance with paragraph 7 below, a United Nations Operation in Somalia (UNOSOM);

3. Requests the Secretary-General immediately to deploy a unit of 50 United Nations Observers to monitor the cease-fire in Mogadishu in accordance with paragraphs 24–26 of the Secretary-General's report (S/23829);

4. Agrees, in principle, also to establish under the overall direction of the Secretary-General's Special Representative a United Nations security force to be deployed as soon as possible to perform the functions described in paragraphs 27–29 of the Secretary-General's report (S/23829);

5. Further requests the Secretary-General to continue his consultations with the parties in Mogadishu regarding the proposed United Nations security

force and, in light of those consultations, to submit his further recommendations to the Security Council for its decision as soon as possible;

6. Welcomes the intention expressed by the Secretary-General in paragraph 64 of his report (S/23829) to appoint a Special Representative for Somalia to provide overall direction of United Nations activities in Somalia and to assist him in his endeavors to reach a peaceful resolution of the conflict in Somalia;

7. Requests the Secretary-General as part of his continuing mission in Somalia to facilitate an immediate and effective cessation of hostilities and the maintenance of a cease-fire throughout the country in order to promote the process of reconciliation and political settlement in Somalia and to provide urgent humanitarian assistance;

8. Welcomes the cooperation between the United Nations and the League of Arab States, the Organization of African Unity, and the Organization of the Islamic Conference in resolving the problem in Somalia;

9. Calls on all parties, movements and factions in Somalia immediately to cease hostilities and to maintain a cease-fire throughout the country in order to promote the process of reconciliation and political settlement in Somalia;

10. Requests the Secretary-General of the United Nations to continue, as a matter of priority, his consultations with all Somali parties, movements and factions towards the convening of a conference for national reconciliation and unity in Somalia in close cooperation with the Organization of African Unity, the League of Arab States and the Organization of the Islamic Conference;

11. Decides to establish, in accordance with rule 28 of the provisional rules of procedure of the Security Council, a Committee of the Security Council consisting of all members of the Council, to undertake the following tasks and to report on its work to the Council with its observations and recommendations:

(a) to seek from all States information regarding the action taken by them concerning the effective implementation of the embargo imposed by paragraph 5 of resolution 733 (1992);

(b) to consider any information brought to its attention by States concerning violations of the embargo, and in that context to make recommendations to the Council on ways of increasing the effectiveness of the embargo;

(c) to recommend appropriate measures in response to violations of the general and complete embargo on all deliveries of weapons and military equipment to Somalia and provide information on a regular basis to the Secretary-General for general distribution to Member States;

12. Notes with appreciation the ongoing efforts of the United Nations, its specialized agencies and humanitarian organizations to ensure delivery of humanitarian assistance to Somalia, particularly to Mogadishu;

13. Calls upon the international community to support, with financial and other resources, the implementation of the 90-day Plan of Action for Emergency Humanitarian Assistance to Somalia;

14. Urges all parties concerned in Somalia to facilitate the efforts of the United Nations, its specialized agencies and humanitarian organizations to provide urgent humanitarian assistance to the affected population in Somalia and reiterates its call for the full respect of the security and safety of the personnel of the humanitarian organizations and the guarantee of their complete freedom of movement in and around Mogadishu and other parts of Somalia;

15. Calls upon all Somali parties, movements and factions to cooperate fully with the Secretary-General in the implementation of the resolution;

16. Decides to remain seized of the matter until a peaceful solution is achieved.

Resolution 767
(adopted 27 July 1992 by unanimous vote)

The Security Council,

Considering the request by Somalia for the Security Council to consider the situation in Somalia (S/23445),

Reaffirming its resolutions 733 (1992) of 23 January 1992, 746 (1992) of 17 March 1992 and 751 (1992) of 24 April 1992,

Having considered the report of the Secretary-General on the situation in Somalia (S/24343),

Considering the letter of the Secretary-General to the President of the Security Council informing him that all the parties in Mogadishu have agreed to the deployment of the 50 military observers, and that the advance party of the observers arrived in Mogadishu on 5 July 1992 and that the rest of the observers arrived in the mission area on 23 July 1992 (S/24179),

Deeply concerned about the availability of arms and ammunition in the hands of civilians and the proliferation of armed banditry throughout Somalia,

Alarmed by the sporadic outbreak of hostilities in several parts of Somalia leading to continued loss of life and destruction of property, and putting at risk the personnel of the United Nations, non-governmental organizations and other humanitarian organizations, as well as disrupting their operations,

Deeply disturbed by the magnitude of the human suffering caused by the conflict and concerned that the situation in Somalia constitutes a grave threat to international peace and security,

Gravely alarmed by the deterioration of the humanitarian situation in Somalia and underlining the urgent need for quick delivery of humanitarian assistance in the whole country,

Recognizing that the provision of humanitarian assistance in Somalia is an important element in the effort of the Council to restore international peace and security in the area,

Responding to the urgent calls by the parties in Somalia for the international community to take measures in Somalia to ensure the delivery of humanitarian assistance in Somalia,

Noting the Secretary-General's proposals for a comprehensive decentralized zonal approach in the United Nations involvement in Somalia,

Cognizant that the success of such an approach requires the cooperation of all parties, movements and factions in Somalia,

1. Takes note with appreciation of the report of the Secretary-General of 22 July 1992 (S/24243);

2. Requests the Secretary-General to make full use of all available means and arrangements, including the mounting of an urgent airlift operation, with a view to facilitating the efforts of the United Nations, its specialized agencies and humanitarian organizations in and accelerating the provision of humanitarian assistance to the affected population in Somalia, threatened by mass starvation;

3. Urges all parties, movements and factions in Somalia to facilitate the efforts of the United Nations, its specialized agencies and humanitarian organizations to provide urgent humanitarian assistance to the affected population in Somalia and reiterates its call for the full respect of the security and safety of the personnel of the humanitarian organizations and the guarantee of their complete freedom of movement in and around Mogadishu and other parts of Somalia;

4. Calls upon all parties, movements and factions in Somalia to cooperate with the United Nations with a view to the urgent deployment of the United Nations security personnel called for in paragraphs 4 and 5 of its resolution 751 (1992), and otherwise assist in the general stabilization

of the situation in Somalia. In the absence of such cooperation, the Security Council does not exclude other measures to deliver humanitarian assistance to Somalia;

5. Reiterates its appeal to the international community to provide adequate financial and other resources for humanitarian efforts in Somalia;

6. Encourages the ongoing efforts of the United Nations, its specialized agencies and humanitarian organizations, including the International Committee of the Red Cross, to ensure delivery of humanitarian assistance to all regions of Somalia;

7. Appeals to all parties, movements and factions in Somalia to extend full cooperation to the military observers and to take measures to ensure their security;

8. Requests the Secretary-General, as part of his continuing efforts in Somalia, to promote an immediate and effective cessation of hostilities and the maintenance of a cease-fire throughout the country in order to facilitate the urgent delivery of humanitarian assistance and the process of reconciliation and political settlement in Somalia;

9. Calls upon all parties, movements and factions in Somalia immediately to cease hostilities and to maintain a cease-fire throughout the country;

10. Stresses the need for the observance and strict monitoring of the general and complete embargo of all deliveries of weapons and military equipment to Somalia, as decided in paragraph 5 of its resolution 733 (1992);

11. Welcomes the cooperation between the United Nations, the Organization of African Unity, the League of Arab States, and the Organization of the Islamic Conference in resolving the situation in Somalia;

12. Approves the Secretary-General's proposal to establish four operations zones in Somalia as part of the consolidated United Nations Operation in Somalia (UNOSOM);

13. Requests the Secretary-General to ensure that his Special Representative for Somalia is provided with all the necessary support services to enable him to effectively carry out his mandate;

14. Strongly supports the Secretary-General's decision urgently to dispatch a technical team to Somalia, under the overall direction of the Special Representative, in order to work within the framework and objectives outlined in paragraph 64 of his report (S/24343) and to submit expeditiously a report to the Security Council on this matter;

15. Affirms that all officials of the United Nations and all experts on mission for the United Nations enjoy the privileges and immunities provided for in the Convention on the Privileges and Immunities of the United Nations of 1946 and in any other relevant instruments and that all parties, movements and factions in Somalia are required to allow them full freedom of movement and all necessary facilities;

16. Requests the Secretary-General to continue urgently his consultations with all parties, movements and factions in Somalia towards the convening of a conference on national reconciliation and unity in Somalia in close cooperation with the Organization of African Unity, the League of Arab States and the Organization of the Islamic Conference;

17. Calls upon all parties, movements and factions in Somalia to cooperate fully with the Secretary-General in the implementation of this resolution;

18. Decides to remain seized of the matter until a peaceful solution is achieved.

Resolution 775
(adopted 28 August 1992 by unanimous vote)

The Security Council,

Considering the request by Somalia for the Security Council to consider the situation in Somalia (S/23445),

Reaffirming its resolutions 733 (1992) of 23 January 1992, 746 (1992) of 17 March 1992, 751 (1992) of 24 April 1992 and 767 (1992) of 27 July 1992,

Having considered the report of the Secretary-General on the situation in Somalia (S/24480),

Deeply concerned about the availability of arms and ammunition and the proliferation of armed banditry throughout Somalia,

Alarmed by the continued sporadic outbreak of hostilities in several parts of Somalia leading to continued loss of life and destruction of property, and putting at risk the personnel of the United Nations, non-governmental organizations and other international humanitarian organizations, as well as disrupting their operations,

Deeply disturbed by the magnitude of the human suffering caused by the conflict and concerned that the situation in Somalia constitutes a threat to international peace and security,

Gravely alarmed by the deterioration of the humanitarian situation in Somalia and underlining the urgent need for quick delivery of humanitarian assistance in the whole country,

Reaffirming that the provision of humanitarian assistance in Somalia is an important element in the effort of the Council to restore international peace and security in the area,

Welcoming the ongoing efforts by the United Nations organizations as well as the International Committee of the Red Cross (ICRC), non-governmental organizations and States to provide humanitarian assistance to the affected population in Somalia,

Welcoming in particular the initiatives to provide relief through airlift operations,

Convinced that no durable progress will be achieved in the absence of an overall political solution to Somalia,

Taking note in particular of paragraph 24 of the report of the Secretary-General,

1. Takes note with appreciation of the report of the Secretary-General of 24 August 1992 (S/24480) on the findings of the technical team and the recommendations of the Secretary-General contained therein;

2. Invites the Secretary-General to establish four zone headquarters as proposed in paragraph 31 of the Secretary-General's report (S/24480);

3. Authorizes the increase in strength of the United Nations Operation in Somalia (UNOSOM) and the subsequent deployment as recommended in paragraph 37 of the Secretary-General's report;

4. Welcomes the decision of the Secretary-General to increase substantially the airlift operation to areas of priority attention;

5. Calls upon all parties, movements and factions in Somalia to cooperate with the United Nations with a view to the urgent deployment of the United Nations security personnel called for in paragraphs 4 and 5 of its resolution 751 (1992) and as recommended in paragraph 37 of the Secretary-General's report;

6. Welcomes all the material and logistical support from a number of States and urges that the airlift operation be effectively coordinated by

the United Nations as described in paragraphs 17 and 21 of the report of the Secretary-General;

7. Urges all parties, movements and factions in Somalia to facilitate the efforts of the United Nations, its specialized agencies and humanitarian organizations to provide urgent humanitarian assistance to the affected population in Somalia and reiterates its call for the full respect of the security and safety of the personnel of these organizations and the guarantee of their complete freedom of movement in and around Mogadishu and other parts of Somalia;

8. Reiterates its appeal to the international community to provide adequate financial and other resources for humanitarian efforts in Somalia;

9. Encourages ongoing efforts of the United Nations, its specialized agencies and humanitarian organizations including the International Committee of the Red Cross and non-governmental organizations to ensure delivery of humanitarian assistance to all regions of Somalia and underlines the importance of coordination between these efforts;

10. Requests also the Secretary-General to continue, in close cooperation with the Organization of African Unity, the League of Arab States and the Organization of the Islamic Conference, his efforts to seek a comprehensive political solution to the crisis in Somalia;

11. Calls upon all parties, movements and factions in Somalia immediately to cease hostilities and to maintain a cease-fire throughout the country;

12. Stresses the need for the observance and strict monitoring of the general and complete embargo on all deliveries of weapons and military equipment to Somalia, as decided in paragraph 5 of its resolution 733 (1992);

13. Calls upon all parties, movements, and factions in Somalia to cooperate fully with the Secretary-General in the implementation of this resolution;

14. Decides to remain seized of the matter until a peaceful resolution is achieved.

Resolution 794
(adopted 3 December 1992 by unanimous vote)

The Security Council,

Reaffirming its resolutions 733 (1992) of 23 January 1992, 746 (1992) of 17 March 1992, 751 (1992) of 24 April 1992 and 767 (1992) of 27 July 1992, and 775 (1992) of 28 August 1992,

Recognizing the unique character of the present situation in Somalia and mindful of its deteriorating, complex and extraordinary nature, requiring an immediate and exceptional response,

Determining that the magnitude of the human tragedy caused by the conflict in Somalia, further exacerbated by the obstacles being created to the distribution of humanitarian assistance, constitutes a threat to international peace and security,

Gravely alarmed by the deterioration of the humanitarian situation in Somalia and underlining the urgent need for the quick delivery of humanitarian assistance to the whole country,

Noting the efforts of the League of Arab States, the Organization of African Unity, and in particular the proposal made by its Assembly for the organization of an international conference on Somalia, and the Organization of the Islamic Conference and other regional agencies and arrangements to promote reconciliation and political settlement in Somalia and to address the humanitarian needs of the people of that country,

Commending the ongoing efforts of the United Nations, its specialized agencies and humanitarian organizations and of non-governmental organizations and of States to ensure delivery of humanitarian assistance in Somalia,

Responding to the urgent calls from Somalia for the international community to take measures to ensure the delivery of humanitarian assistance in Somalia,

Expressing grave alarm at continuing reports of widespread violations of international humanitarian law occurring in Somalia, including violence and threats of violence against personnel participating lawfully in impartial humanitarian relief activities; deliberate attacks on noncombatants, relief consignments and vehicles, and medical and relief facilities; and impeding the delivery of food and medical supplies essential for the survival of the civilian population,

Dismayed by the continuation of conditions that impede the delivery of humanitarian supplies to destinations within Somalia, and in particular reports of looting of relief supplies destined for starving people, attacks on aircraft and ships bringing in humanitarian relief supplies, and attacks on the Pakistani UNOSOM contingent in Mogadishu,

Taking note with appreciation of the letters of the Secretary-General of 24 November 1992 (S/24859) and of 29 November 1992 (S/24868),

Sharing the Secretary-General's assessment that the situation in Somalia is intolerable and that it has become necessary to review the basic principles and premises of the United Nations efforts in Somalia, and that UNOSOM's existing course would not in present circumstances be an adequate response to the tragedy in Somalia,

Determined to establish as soon as possible the necessary conditions for the delivery of humanitarian assistance wherever needed in Somalia, in conformity with resolutions 751 (1992) and 767 (1992),

Noting the offer by Member States aimed at establishing a secure environment for humanitarian relief operations in Somalia as soon as possible,

Determined further to restore peace, stability and law and order with a view to facilitating the process of a political settlement under the auspices of the United Nations, aimed at national reconciliation in Somalia, and encouraging the Secretary-General and his Special Representative to continue and intensify their work at the national and regional levels to promote these objectives,

Recognizing that the people of Somalia bear ultimate responsibility for their national reconciliation and the reconstruction of their own country,

1. Reaffirms its demand that all parties, movements and factions in Somalia immediately cease hostilities, maintain a cease-fire throughout the country, and cooperate with the Special Representative of the Secretary-General as well as with the military forces to be established pursuant to the authorization given in paragraph 10 below in order to promote the process of relief distribution, reconciliation and political settlement in Somalia;

2. Demands that all parties, movements and factions in Somalia take all measures necessary to facilitate the efforts of the United Nations, its specialized agencies and humanitarian organizations to provide urgent humanitarian assistance to the affected population in Somalia;

3. Also demands that all parties, movements and factions in Somalia take all measures necessary to ensure the safety of United Nations and all other personnel engaged in the delivery of humanitarian assistance, including the military forces to be established pursuant to the authorization given in paragraph 10 below;

4. Further demands that all parties, movements and factions in Somalia immediately cease and desist from all breaches of international humanitarian law including from actions such as those described above;

5. Strongly condemns all violations of international humanitarian law occurring in Somalia, including in particular the deliberate impeding of the delivery of food and medical supplies essential for the survival of the civilian population, and affirms that those who commit or order

the commission of such acts will be held individually responsible in respect of such acts;

6. Decides that the operations and the further deployment of the 3,500 personnel of the United Nations Operation in Somalia (UNOSOM) authorized by paragraph 3 of resolution 775 (1992) should proceed at the discretion of the Secretary-General in the light of his assessment of conditions on the ground; and requests him to keep the Council informed and to make such recommendations as may be appropriate for the fulfillment of its mandate where conditions permit;

7. Endorses the recommendations by the Secretary-General in his letter of 29 November 1992 (S/24868) that action under Chapter VII of the Charter of the United Nations should be taken in order to establish a secure environment for humanitarian relief operations in Somalia as soon as possible;

8. Welcomes the offer by a Member State described in the Secretary-General's letter to the Council of 29 November 1992 (S/24868) concerning the establishment of an operation to create such a secure environment;

9. Welcomes also offers by other Member States to participate in that operation;

10. Acting under Chapter VII of the Charter of the United Nations, authorizes the Secretary-General and Member States cooperating to implement the offer referred to in paragraph 8 above to use all necessary means to establish as soon as possible a secure environment for humanitarian relief operations in Somalia;

11. Calls on all Member States which are in a position to do so to provide military forces and to make additional contributions, in cash or kind, in accordance with paragraph 10 above and requests the Secretary-General to establish a fund through which the contributions, where appropriate, could be channelled to the States or operations concerned;

12. Authorizes the Secretary-General and the Member States concerned to make the necessary arrangements for the unified command and control of the forces involved, which will reflect the offer referred to in paragraph 8 above;

13. Requests the Secretary-General and the Member States acting under paragraph 10 above to establish appropriate mechanisms for coordination between the United Nations and their military forces;

14. Decides to appoint an ad hoc commission composed of members of the Security Council to report to the Council on the implementation of this resolution;

15. Invites the Secretary-General to attach a small UNOSOM liaison staff to the Field Headquarters of the unified command;

16. Acting under Chapters VII and VIII of the Charter, calls upon States, nationally or through regional agencies or arrangements, to use such measures as may be necessary to ensure strict implementation of paragraph 5 of resolution 733 (1992);

17. Requests all States, in particular those in the region, to provide appropriate support for the actions undertaken by States, nationally or through regional agencies or arrangements, pursuant to this and other relevant resolutions;

18. Requests the Secretary-General and, as appropriate, the States concerned to report to the Council on a regular basis, the first such report to be made no later than fifteen days after the adoption of this resolution, on the implementation of this resolution and the attainment of the objective of establishing a secure environment so as to enable the Council to make the necessary decision for a prompt transition to continued peace-keeping operations;

19. Requests the Secretary-General to submit a plan to the Council initially within fifteen days after the adoption of this resolution to

ensure that UNOSOM will be able to fulfil its mandate upon the withdrawal of the unified command;

20. Invites the Secretary-General and his Special Representative to continue their efforts to achieve a political settlement in Somalia;

21. Decides to remain actively seized of the matter.

NOTES

1. For some discussion of the political situation before 1988 see Richard Greenfield, "An Embattled Barre," *Africa Report*, May/June 1987, 65–69; and Anthony Shaw, "Barre's Balancing Act," *Africa Report*, November/December 1985, 26–29.

2. See Greenfield, "An Embattled Barre," 65. See appendix A for an outline of Somali clans and political parties.

3. See Christopher Clapham, "The Political Economy of Conflict in the Horn of Africa," *Survival* 23, no. 5 (September/October 1990): 403–419.

4. See Richard Greenfield, "Barre's Unholy Alliances," *Africa Report*, March/April 1989, 66.

5. See Peter Schraeder, "The Horn of Africa: U.S. Foreign Policy in an Altered Cold War Environment," *Middle East Journal* 46, no. 4 (Autumn 1992): 574; for more information on Somali atrocities, see "Bloody Somalia," *The Nation*, June 25, 1988, 884–885.

6. Destruction in the north of Somalia is documented in the UN report *The Situation in Somalia, Report of the Secretary-General*, S/23829/Add.1, April 21, 1992.

7. See Linda Feldman, "Rebels Create Havoc for U.S.-Backed Somalia," *Christian Science Monitor*, July 6, 1988, 1.

8. Robert M. Press, "Africa Watch Report Sounds Alarm on Somalia," *Christian Science Monitor*, January 18, 1990, 5.

9. See Amnesty International, *A Long Term Human Rights Crisis* (London: Amnesty International Publications, 1988); Robert Gersony, *Why Somalis Flee: Synthesis of Accounts of Conflict Experience in Northern Somalia by Somali Refugees, Displaced Persons, and Others* (Washington, D.C.: Bureau for Displaced Persons, U.S. Department of State, 1989); U.S. General Accounting Office, *Somalia: Observations Regarding the Northern Conflict and Resulting Conditions* (Washington, D.C.: U.S. General Accounting Office, 1989); Africa Watch, *Somalia: A*

Government at War with Its Own People: Testimonies about Killings and the Conflict in the North (London: Africa Watch, 1990).

10. Robert M. Press, "Somali Dissidents Detail Government Wrongdoings," *Christian Science Monitor,* December 31, 1990, 6.

11. "Somalia: Dissent," *Africa Confidential* 31, no. 12 (June 15, 1990).

12. Press, "Somali Dissidents," 6.

13. Abdul Mohammed, "Power Games in Africa's Horn," *New York Times,* July 11, 1990, A19.

14. The United States could have done more to mediate the conflict had it taken an interest in it. In fact, on June 4, 1988, the Somalis requested an air shipment of previously authorized military aid that included 1,200 M-16 rifles and 2.8 million rounds of ammunition. The Department of Defense routinely shipped the materiel. See Schraeder, 575–576.

15. Linda Feldman, "Somalia's U.S.-Backed Leader Shaken," *Christian Science Monitor*, July 28, 1988.

16. "The Mayor of Mogadishu," *The Economist*, September 29, 1990, 47.

17. See "Raid on Fuel Depot Near Somali Capital Said to Kill Dozens," *New York Times*, December 29, 1990, A3.

18. Jane Perlez, "U.S. and Italy Evacuating Foreigners in Somalia," *New York Times*, January 6, 1991, A3.

19. See Robert M. Press, "Somalia's Leaders Look for Ways to Keep the Peace," *Christian Science Monitor*, February 5, 1991, 4.

20. For more on the clans see Robert M. Press, "Solutions to Somalia's Crisis Center on Trust Between Clans," *Christian Science Monitor,* September 21, 1992.

21. Peter Biles, "Starting from Scratch," *Africa Report,* May/June 1991, 55–59.

22. Jane Perlez, "Somali Forces Clash with Rebels for 3rd Day as Both Report Gains," *New York Times*, January 2, 1991, 3.

23. For more on the absence of the UN from Somalia, see Tony P. Hall, "The United Nations Must Return to Somalia," *Christian Science Monitor*, March 13, 1992, 19.

24. Robert M. Press, "After Dictator's Ouster, Somalis Face Hunger," *Christian Science Monitor*, February 11, 1991, 6.

25. See *Press Conference by Médicines sans Frontières on Aid to Somalia*, United Nations Information Center Files, Washington, D.C., January 30, 1992.

26. Robert M. Press, "Somali Civil War Takes Stiff Toll on Civilians," *Christian Science Monitor,* December 16, 1991, 8. On U.S. aid see also Jane Perlez, "U.S. Increases Aid to Somalia After U.N. Balks," *New York Times*, December 15, 1991, 6.

27. See Schraeder, 583–584.

28. Ibid.

29. "Somalia: Still Fighting," *Africa Confidential* 32, no. 16 (August 9, 1991): 6.

30. "Somalia: Fragile Agreements," *Africa Confidential* 32, no. 21 (October 25, 1991): 5.

31. Note Jonathan Stevenson's comments on the UN in this regard in "Hope Restored in Somalia?" *Foreign Policy* 91: 144.

32. On the fighting in Mogadishu see Jane Perlez, "Somalia Self-Destructs and the World Looks On," *New York Times*, December 29, 1991, IV: 4; "Hundreds Slain in 5th Day of Strife in Somalia," *New York Times*, November 22, 1991, 9; and "Foes Step Up Artillery Duels in Somalia's Capital," *New York Times,* November 24, 1991, 11.

33. Jane Perlez, "UN Sees Danger of Somali Famine," *New York Times*, February 27, 1992, A3. See also *Situation in Somalia*, April 21, 1992. A joint report by Africa Watch and Physicians for Human Rights estimated that 14,000 people were killed and 27,000 wounded in Mogadishu between November 1991 and February 1992.

34. See "Somalia: UN Cease-Fire Ignored," *Africa Research Bulletin*, February 1992, 10472.

35. Perlez, "Danger of Somali Famine."

36. *UN Chronicle*, June 1992, 23.

37. See Jane Perlez, "Warring Somalia Factions Agree to Meet at UN," *New York Times,* February 8, 1992, 2, and Robert M. Press, "UN to Monitor Somalia Cease Fire," *Christian Science Monitor*, March 5, 1992, 3.

38. See Robert M. Press and Lucia Mouat, "United Nations Takes Lead in Somalia Crisis," *Christian Science Monitor*, February 12, 1992, 6.

39. Another tragedy was that 200,000 Ethiopians who had fled to Somalia in the early 1980s were now forced back into Ethiopia and "homeless in their own country." See Robert M. Press, "Somalis are Trapped by Two Wars," *Christian Science Monitor*, June 11, 1991, 5.

40. For more information on refugees see Dennis Gallagher and Susan Forbes Martin, *The Many Faces of the Somali Crisis: Humanitarian Issues in Somalia, Kenya, and Ethiopia* (Washington, D.C.: Refugee Policy Group, 1992).

41. For more information see *Situation in Somalia*, April 21, 1992.

42. See Stevenson, 145–146.

43. For one account of the mood in Mogadishu in these days see Biles, "Starting from Scratch."

44. See Mohamoud A. Afrah, *Target: Villa Somalia, An Eyewitness Account of Mogadishu's Fall to U.S.C. Guerillas* (Karachi: Naseem, 1991).

45. See "Somalia: Time to Take Stock," *Africa Confidential* 33, no. 8 (April 17, 1992): 4.

46. Quoted in Peter Biles, "Anarchy Rules," *Africa Report*, July/August 1992, 32.

47. On the UN and its problems see Robert M. Press, "UN Responds to Critics on Somalia," *Christian Science Monitor*, September 2, 1992; and Scott Peterson, "Aid Workers on the Ground Deplore Bureaucratic Delay," *Christian Science Monitor*, September 2, 1992.

48. Jane Perlez, "UN Let the Somali Famine Get Out of Hand, Aide Says," *New York Times*, August 16, 1992, A12.

49. For a discussion of ICRC efforts in Somalia and throughout Africa see Jane Perlez, "In Africa's War Zones, More of the Red Cross," *New York Times*, April 28, 1991, 6, and "Somalia: The Politics of Hunger," *Africa Confidential* 33, no. 19 (September 1992): 3.

50. "Death by Looting," *The Economist,* July 18, 1992, 41.

51. Mohamed Sahnoun, *Report to the United Nations Secretary-General: Somalia, May–June 1992* (June 25, 1992): 7–9.

52. All figures come from the World Food Program, *Update on Humanitarian Assistance: Somalia* (New York: United Nations, 1993).

53. See Scott Peterson, "World Shifts Attention to Somalia," *Christian Science Monitor*, September 2, 1992, 1.

54. *The Situation in Somalia, Report of the Secretary-General,* S/24480, August 24, 1992.

55. See "Somalia: Third of Country Faces Death," *Africa Research Bulletin,* July 1992, 10663.

56. Hence my surprise to receive a message from the secretary-general a few days later directing us to refrain from any criticism of UN agencies' work. Apparently my statement at the October 12 meeting led some agencies to complain to the secretary-general.

57. Paul Lewis, "U.S. Offering a Plan for Somali Relief," *New York Times,* September 18, 1992, A10.

58. See article by Ray Bonner in *Mother Jones* (March/April 1993). It happens sometimes that a UN agency will overbid another UN agency for the rent of a facility or the use of a service.

59. These unarmed military observers were of different nationalities, each wearing their own national uniform. Their mandate was to monitor the cease-fire along the dividing line in Mogadishu.

60. See articles by Ray Bonner in *Mother Jones* (March/April 1993) and Jonathan Stevenson in *Foreign Policy* (Summer 1993).

61. Alan James, "The Equality of States: Contemporary Manifestations of an Ancient Doctrine," *Review of International Studies* 18 (1992): 377–391.

62. See Alan James, *Sovereign Statehood: The Basis of International Society* (London: Allen and Unwin, 1990): 25–30. James notes that nonsovereign states can also play an international role, but this is an exception to the rule.

63. James, "Equality of States," 384.

64. David J. Scheffer, "Humanitarian Intervention versus State Sovereignty," in *Peacemaking and Peacekeeping: Implications for the United States Military* (Washington, D.C.: United States Institute of Peace, 1993): 13–14.

65. Quoted in David J. Scheffer, "Challenges Confronting Collective Security: Humanitarian Intervention," in David J. Scheffer, Richard N. Gardner, and Gerald B. Helman, *Three Views on the Issue of Humanitarian Intervention* (Washington, D.C.: United States Institute of Peace, 1992): 4.

66. Boutros Boutros-Ghali, *An Agenda for Peace*, a report of the secretary-general pursuant to the statement adopted by the summit meeting of the Security Council on January 31, 1992 (June 17, 1992): 5.

67. Margaret A. Novicki, "Interview: A New Agenda for the OAU—Salim Ahmed Salim," *Africa Report*, May/June 1992, 37.

68. United Nations, *Review of the 100-Day Programme and Beyond: Key Issues*, United Nations Information Center, Somalia File, 1.

69. Ibid., 2.

70. For a description of the deteriorating security conditions see Jane Perlez, "UN Relief Official in Somalia Quits in Dispute with Headquarters," *New York Times*, October 28, 1992, A6.

71. See Mark Huband, "When Yankee Goes Home," *Africa Report*, March/April 1993, 21; and Jane Perlez, "Thievery and Extortion Halt Flow of UN Food to Somalis," *New York Times*, December 1, 1992, A1.

72. Secretary-General Boutros-Ghali to Andre Erdos, president of the Security Council (United Nations Information Center Files, Washington, D.C.), November 29, 1992, 3.

73. On the same day Secretary-General Boutros-Ghali was drafting his letter, a World Food Program ship carrying 10,000 tons of food was shelled as it attempted to dock at Mogadishu. For more information on the UN deliberations see Paul Lewis, "UN Chief Requests New Force to Ease Somalia's Misery Now," *New York Times*, December 1, 1992, A1; and "U.S. Commits Force to Somalia, But for How Long?" *Africa Report*, January/February 1992, 5.

74. See the London *Sunday Times*, August 15, 1993.

INDEX

United States Institute of Peace

The United States Institute of Peace is an independent, nonpartisan federal institution created and funded by Congress to strengthen the nation's capacity to promote the peaceful resolution of international conflict. Established in 1984, the Institute meets its congressional mandate through an array of programs, including grants, fellowships, conferences and workshops, library services, publications, and other educational activities. The Institute's Board of Directors is appointed by the President of the United States and confirmed by the Senate.

Board of Directors

Jennings Randolph Program for International Peace

As part of the statute establishing the United States Institute of Peace, Congress envisioned a fellowship program that would appoint "scholars and leaders of peace from the United States and abroad to pursue scholarly inquiry and other appropriate forms of communication on international peace and conflict resolution." The program was named after Senator Jennings Randolph of West Virginia, whose efforts over four decades helped to establish the Institute.

Since it began in 1987, the Jennings Randolph Program has played a key role in the Institute's effort to build a national center of research, dialogue, and education on critical problems of conflict and peace. Through a rigorous annual competition, outstanding men and women from diverse nations and fields are selected to carry out projects designed to expand and disseminate knowledge on violent international conflict and the wide range of ways it can be peacefully managed or resolved.

The Institute's Distinguished Fellows and Peace Fellows are individuals from a wide variety of academic and other professional backgrounds who work at the Institute on research and education projects they have proposed and participate in the Institute's collegial and public outreach activities. The Institute's Peace Scholars are doctoral candidates at American universities who are working on their dissertations.

Institute fellows and scholars have worked on such varied subjects as international negotiation, regional security arrangements, conflict resolution techniques, international legal systems, ethnic and religious conflict, arms control, and the protection of human rights, and these issues have been examined in settings throughout the world.

As part of its effort to disseminate original and useful analyses of peace and conflict to policymakers and the public, the Institute publishes book manuscripts and other written products that result from the fellowship work and meet the Institute's high standards of quality.

Joseph Klaits
Acting Director

SOMALIA
THE MISSED OPPORTUNITIES

The text of this book was set in Berkeley Old Style; the display type is Laudatio. Cover design by Laurie Rosenthal of Meadows and Wiser; cover photo courtesy of Betty H. Press. Interior design by Joan Engelhardt and Day Wilkes Dosch; map prepared by Marie Marr-Williams; page makeup by Helene Y. Redmond of HYR Graphics.